# Tabula Plena

## Forms of Urban P

# Tabula Plena

## Forms of Urban Preservation

**Edited by Bryony Roberts**

Oslo School of Architecture and Design
Columbia University GSAPP
**Lars Müller Publishers**

**Tabula Plena: Forms of Urban Preservation**

Editor: Bryony Roberts
Proofreading: Rita Forbes
Design: Jessica Fleischmann / still room
Production assistance: Dorothy Lin / still room
Diagrams: Shiqing Liu
Assistance: Ida Nordstrøm

Printing and binding: Kösel, Altusried-Krugzell, Germany
Paper: 130 g/sm Munken Lynx
Typefaces: Maison Neue, Neuzeit Grotesk, Atlas Grotesk

Lars Müller Publishers
Zurich, Switzerland
www.lars-mueller-publishers.com

ISBN 978-3-03778-491-4


Printed in Germany

Cover: The government quarter, Oslo, 1969–72 (photo: Teigens Fotoatelier / DEXTRA Photo, Teknisk museum),
overlaid with Open Quarter, analytical plan, Helle Bendixen and Bryony Roberts, AHO and GSAPP Team, 2015

## Acknowledgments

This publication is made possible by the generous support of the Oslo School of Architecture and Design (AHO) and Columbia University Graduate School of Architecture, Planning and Preservation (GSAPP). Many thanks to Dean Ole Gustavsen of AHO, Dean Mark Wigley of GSAPP, and Dean Amale Andraos of GSAPP for enthusiastically supporting both this book and the project for the Oslo government quarter.

A result of many collaborative courses, projects, and conversations, this book would not be possible without the dedication and creativity of the students and faculty of AHO and GSAPP. Thanks to not only the direct collaborators, but also to the critics who offered questions and insights: Thordis Arrhenius, Sarah Whiting, Gro Bonesmo, Hege Maria Eriksson, Linda Veiby, Marianne Skjulhaug, Elisabeth Sjødahl, Erling Dokk Holm, Janne Wilberg, Even Smith Wergeland, and Kjetil Thorsen.

Special thanks to Statsbygg for including the AHO and GSAPP team in the government planning process, and to Deichmanske Library for enabling us to showcase this work to the city.

Contents

# Agency

# Form

# Case Study

# Pedagogy

# Addendum

Y-blokka building, Government quarter, Oslo

# Introduction

**Bryony Roberts**

Three years after a terrorist bombing on July 22, 2011, the national government quarter of Oslo remained half-empty. The two central, modernist buildings designed by Erling Viksjø—the Høyblokka and Y-blokka—were cleared of debris but left mostly vacant due to ongoing debates over memorialization and future planning. In late 2014 and early 2015, the Norwegian government initiated a planning process to transform the site, mandating the demolition of the Y-blokka, part of the Høyblokka, and several surrounding buildings to build new office towers. This unilateral decision, in a culture that values democratic consensus, enraged not only architects and preservationists but also the larger Norwegian population. Decisions about demolition or preservation took on great political significance, as they impacted not only specific buildings, but also experiences of remembrance and representations of national government. Yet, the planning process staged an unproductive opposition between the interests of architectural preservation and urban growth. Associated with the defense of historical monuments, preservation was seen as tangential to the issue of densification. The process foregrounded the need to connect the fields of preservation, architecture, and urban planning, and to position preservation as a design discipline capable of integrating historical and new architecture at the urban scale.

Entering this fray, a collaborative team from the Oslo School of Architecture and Design (AHO) and Columbia University Graduate School of Architecture, Planning, and Preservation (GSAPP) joined the ideas phase of the official planning process alongside six professional teams. While the other teams accepted the government's plans for demolition, this academic team, which I led in consultation with Erik Langdalen of AHO and Jorge Otero-Pailos of GSAPP, rejected those conditions and offered strategies for combining the historical buildings with new construction. Beyond the specifics of the Oslo government site or the design proposal, this collaboration also aimed to challenge the disciplinary boundaries between architecture, preservation, and urban planning. Growing from that project, this book expands the conversation further, examining how collaboration among the disciplines can introduce alternative modes of political agency and architectural design.

In contrast to the *tabula rasa* approach favored by many of the professional teams in the planning process, our team pursued the possibilities of *tabula plena*. A familiar term in both architecture and urbanism, *tabula rasa* evokes not only its etymological origins in ancient wax tablets melted clean, but also, more recently, the clearing of urban sites for late modernist urban renewal. Both a scathing critique and a secret fantasy, the term conjures the freedom of operating without the constraints of existing conditions. In contrast, *tabula plena*, a term used by Otero-Pailos during discussions in Oslo, connotes urban sites full of existing buildings from different time periods.[1] The phrase literally means a full tablet; a space where a density of previous markings remains. But moving beyond the metaphor of architecture as writing and the evocation of palimpsests, we can look to the alternative definitions of tabula as a game board or table. *Tabula plena* then doubles as a game board left in mid-play, with the pieces mapping out strategies and ambitions, or to stretch the Latin further, a table after a dinner party, with the complex arrangements of plates, glasses, and silverware positioned by a series of social negotiations. In either case, the condition of found objects offers an invitation to rearrange.

Strategies for responding to *tabula plena* conditions are becoming increasingly urgent. The accumulation of existing building stock and the importance of sustainability have intensified the need for reuse and preservation projects. Developing smart strategies for existing buildings requires not only governmental support— through changes to economic incentives, zoning policies, and environmental regulations— but also creative and intellectual engagement by architects and preservationists. While high-profile projects such as Herzog + de Meuron's Caixa Forum in Madrid and Diller Scofidio + Renfro's Alice Tully Hall in New York have attracted media attention, there remains a vacuum in architectural education and discourse around reuse projects. New strategies for modifying *tabula plena* require exchanges among the fields of architecture, preservation, and urban planning, which are currently siloed in distinct disciplines. What is needed — in discourse, education, and practice — is an exploration of the architectural and political ramifications of transforming sites dense with existing structures.

While earlier discourses on preservation and contextualism provide important reference points, they fall short of offering guidance for modifying contemporary urban sites. Despite the long history of altering existing structures around the world, current preservation discourse focuses on the protection of singular monuments over the transformation of urban structures. As detailed by Jukka Jokilehto in *A History of Architectural Conservation*, [2] actions of repairing and protecting cultural monuments have been ongoing since antiquity, with evidence from ancient Egyptian, Greek, and Roman cultures. In the ensuing centuries of political, economic, and religious transitions, practices of maintaining culturally significant buildings have included a wide range of activities from repair to addition to reconstruction. In reaction to willful restorations such as those of Eugène-Emmanuel Viollet-le-Duc, however, the western preservation discourse that formed in the late nineteenth and early twentieth century limited alterations and prioritized protection of original materials and authorship. While the progression from the Athens Charter (1931) to the Venice Charter (1964) to the UNESCO Operational Guidelines (1972) expanded the definition of heritage to include urban sites, landscapes, and intangible qualities, the goal still remains to protect original conditions from change. Recent discourses on urban conservation have promoted exchange between preservationists and planners to shape urban growth, but these conversations do not closely examine the implications for architectural design.

In the fields of architecture and urbanism, the discourses from the 1950s through the 1970s, which often arose in reaction to *tabula rasa* modernism, have loomed the largest in contemporary engagement with existing conditions. This era fostered discourses on modification (Vittorio Gregotti, Ernesto Rogers), typology (Aldo Rossi, Rafael Moneo, Rob and Léon Krier), bricolage (Colin Rowe), and façadism (Robert Venturi and Denise Scott Brown). But while sophisticated in their theoretical formulations, these strategies have filtered down to everyday practices of façadism — camouflaging new buildings through mimetic scale and material, or decorating functional sheds with ironic historical references. The contemporary surge in reuse and preservation projects, while sometimes repeating tropes of façadism, is also demanding and opening up alternative forms of practice. The increasing interdependence of the fields of architecture and preservation introduces possibilities for more collaborative, political agency and a relational design process.

Collaborations among architects, preservationists, and urban planners have the potential to shift conceptions of both design authorship and architectural form. Processes of alteration and reuse necessarily challenge the concept of signature authorship. They prompt architects to work in response to previous architects' decisions, as well as in collaboration with preservationists, planners, structural engineers, and community interests. Such collaborations also pull preservationists away from positions of seeming objectivity into roles with more explicit authorship, as they make choices about what to preserve and how to frame it for contemporary audiences. As a result, architects and preservationists both participate in a different form of design, producing architecture in response to political, economic, and aesthetic valuations of a site. They step into the *tabula plena* game board mid-play, responding to the decisions of their collaborators and those who have acted before. This interactive process also challenges expectations for architectural form. Through processes of enhancing, extending, or erasing, architects and preservationists generate architectural forms that emerge directly from existing structures and are sometimes only partially visible. These projects introduce different definitions of coherence in architecture, particularly at the urban scale, where they operate across multiple buildings of different time periods.

Expanding on these questions of authorship and architectural form, this book points to the theoretical implications and design possibilities of engaging *tabula plena* conditions. The book stages a loose dialogue between texts and projects, bringing together short manifestos, design precedents, and discussions on pedagogy, along with the case study of the Oslo government quarter. The Agency section — a collection of short essays by scholars and practitioners — examines the politics of collaboration between architects, preservationists, and community interests. Addressing this different model of architectural authorship, Jorge Otero-Pailos discusses how the design of supplementary structures turns historical remains into "monumentaries." Daniel Abramson considers the changing relations between architectural practice and time, arguing for the benefits of designing for obsolescence. Practitioners Eduardo Rojas and Elizabeth Timme both address the challenge of involving community interests in transforming existing sites; the former through discussing structures of governance and the latter through questioning how to moderate community participation. Reflecting on the shift towards reuse projects in architecture firms known for iconic new buildings, Ippolito Pestellini Laparelli of OMA discusses the virtues of abstinence and Winy Maas of MVRDV argues for architectural diversity. Providing a critical counterpoint to the celebration of authorship in preservation, Salvador Muñoz Viñas connects Roland Barthes' "The Death of the Author" to current preservation discourse, and Christian Parreno questions how preservation serves to reinforce political authority.

The second section, Form, explores how dense urban sites prompt alternative approaches to architectural form. Working with multiple existing buildings prompts different definitions of part-to-whole relationships. Architects and preservationists must determine the degree to which different buildings can be read or experienced as a whole. Formatted as an index of formal strategies, this section highlights different approaches to generating coherence at the scale of the site. In contrast to strategies of contextual mimesis or façadist preservation, which maintain the appearance of stasis, all of these projects reveal the volumetric transformation of a historical site. In the trajectory of projects from the 1960s to the present, we see a range of strategies for producing part-to-whole relations. From the 1960s, Yona Friedman's Ville Spatiale and Candilis Josic Woods' reconstruction of Frankfurt-Römerberg reposition historical structures within larger megastructures. Seen in this context, Superstudio's Continuous Monument can be read as a suggestion for unusual site-specificity, through the collision of a monolith with the Manhattan skyline. Lina Bo Bardi's SESC Pompéia counterbalances these megastructures with a composite of disparate volumes, while Bernard Tschumi's Fresnoy Art Center introduces an overarching envelope that produces interstitial social spaces. In more recent work by Xaveer de Geyter Architects, Mansilla + Tuñón, and José María Sánchez García Arquitectos, strong and highly legible Platonic forms tie together multiple existing buildings. OMA's recent Fondazione Prada offers a playful inversion of the trope of façadism, while Pier Vittorio Aureli, known for his advocacy of autonomy, reveals new designs for the reuse of postwar commercial buildings. Finally, MVRDV's proposal for the Oslo government quarter provokes both preservation conventions and the representation of political identity.

The third section — Case Study — looks specifically at the collaborative master plan for the Oslo government quarter produced by the Oslo School of Architecture and Design and the Columbia University GSAPP. The academic team of masters students, PhD students, and professors took an activist approach, challenging the government's plans for demolition and proposing a strategy for combining preservation and urban growth. Erik Langdalen discusses the importance of urban conservation in the evolution of the site, and argues for the political significance of historical diversity in representations of governance. Unpacking the politics of the government quarter and the planning process, architectural historian Mattias Ekman discusses how mediated depictions of the site in newspapers and television shaped decisions about preservation.

Building from this project, the book addresses how educational pedagogy in both architecture and preservation can cultivate strategies for engaging *tabula plena* sites. The fourth section, Pedagogy, includes a manifesto by Thordis Arrhenius on teaching both analysis and alteration of the existing as a creative practice, followed by a discussion that I moderated between Thordis Arrhenius, Jorge Otero-Pailos, and Erik Langdalen about producing crossovers between architecture and preservation programs. A teaching bibliography offers reference texts for introducing students to past and current discourses on alternative preservation. Finally, the Addendum section of the book includes other courses and projects that surrounded this case study, including a fall 2014 studio in Oslo taught by me, Andrea Pinochet, and Laura Saether, and one at Columbia GSAPP taught by Jorge Otero-Pailos and Craig Konyk.

The groundswell of attention on preservation and adaptive reuse over the last several years has made the urgency of these issues clear. But these conversations remain sporadic and marginal. This is an awkward, transitional moment for architecture, in which conceptions of creativity are shifting. Not only are structures of practice changing, from traditional office formats to free-form consulting and freelancing jobs, but architects are increasingly required to operate in response to existing architecture. Rather than denying these changes in practice, continuing to marginalize reuse projects or desperately seeking new approximations of *tabula rasa*, this is a moment to expand these new forms of creativity. Visionary design does not emerge in a vacuum; it grows from the intellectual support system of manifestos, criticism, radical pedagogies, and past precedents. To develop new strategies for engaging *tabula plena* sites requires the construction of an intellectual context. This book gathers conversations already occurring about the theoretical and pedagogical implications of transforming existing buildings, along with design practices producing bold combinations of historical and new architecture, to examine how they are changing conceptions of architectural agency and form. Together, they speak to the potential of remaking contemporary cities and redefining architectural creativity.

### Notes

1     The term *tabula plena* has appeared previously in writings about architecture and urbanism as a counterpoint to *tabula plena*, as in Nan Ellin, "What is Good Urbanism?" in *Emergent Urbanism: Urban Planning and Design in Times of Structural and Systemic Change,* ed. Tigran Haas and Krister Olsson (Surrey: Ashgate, 2014), 102; Nan Ellin, *Good Urbanism* (Washington DC: Island Press, 2012), 15, 16.

2     Jukka Jokilehto, *A History of Architectural Conservation* (London: Routledge, 1999), 4-6.

# Agency

# Monumentaries

## Jorge Otero-Pailos

### 1.

Let me propose the neologism "monumentaries" to describe the notion that monuments are not just material documents of the past, but also the expression of a contemporary editorial point of view. Monumentaries are historical buildings that have been purposefully altered *post facto* in order to influence our perception and conception of them. Any careful observer of historic buildings knows that, in order to keep them standing over the centuries, some measure of alteration is always necessary, but that doesn't make every monument a monumentary. We have to distinguish between alterations due to low-level maintenance, like replacing a couple of shingles to fix a leaky roof, and alterations to express an idea, like replacing a metal roof with clay shingles in order to create a more historically accurate image of the building at the moment of original construction. Only the latter type of alteration, insofar as it is justified by both a technical need *and* an intellectual proposition, is an intentional attempt to turn the monument into a monumentary.

Monumentaries are both material and conceptual objects meant to operate discursively in various social, cultural, and political realms, as well as disciplines such as architecture, art, history, and others. I will focus in particular on the material that is added to monuments in order to transform them into monumentaries. This material, while often presented as a purely functional repair meant to be invisible, or at least dismissible, is in fact a very important aspect of the aesthetics of monumentaries. As a modifying aesthetic, it also operates as a conceptual supplement, able to reconfigure, sometimes slightly, other times completely, the ideas previously associated with the monument. While material supplements to monuments are often intentionally obvious and easy to see, their conceptual status is paradoxically difficult to decipher. Building on Jacques Derrida's analysis of artistic *parerga*, the supplements described in Kantian aesthetics, I will argue that monumentaries are created through supplements that are both the same as and different than those at work in other artworks: the same in the sense that they are conceptually extrinsic to the work, materials that need to be removed in order to appreciate the work, while being indispensable and therefore constitutive of it, and different because they are meant to physically and conceptually protect and preserve the work for the future. What follows is an attempt to refine the concept of the supplement as it pertains to architecture by theorizing the *apergon*, the part of architecture that protects it until it will have been fit to stand on its own, that is to say, fit to be understood.

Restored wall of the ancient Roman theater in Arles, France

## 2.

As in film documentaries, architectural monumentaries must strike a careful balance between staging historical evidence objectively and presenting the filmmaker's or the architect's subjective editorial point of view. In the ruins of the ancient Roman theater of Arles, France, the editorial point of view of the contemporary architect appears as an attempt to present a speculative image of how the ground-level arcade of the theater's façade might have looked when it was originally built in the first century BCE. Pedestrians walking the perimeter of the theater, along the Rue de la Calade, are presented with a white iron fence placed along the exact location where the ancient façade once stood. A few blocks of limestone that were clearly the base of the façade interrupt the fence. As the visitor nears the northwest corner, these blocks rise up and turn into a one-story wall with three arches flanked by Doric pilasters. The limestone ashlar is crisply rendered, suggesting that it was laid more recently, during a major restoration campaign carried out at the end of the nineteenth century, and retouched between 2005 and 2009.

Interestingly, the hand of the new architect, the editorial expression, recedes at key moments — for instance, in the case of the new ashlar that stops short of covering the whole surface of the wall in order to reveal remnants of weathered ancient stones. The new stones frame the historic evidence, staging it for us to appreciate as an "untouched" document of the past. The need to show these original stones cannot be overstated: they are the objective historic documents that legitimate the contemporary work. Yet paradoxically, their status as documents of ancient Rome is not clear *prima facie*. Their deformed shapes and lack of carvings make them partially illegible as historic evidence. The stones alone cannot perform their appointed task as legible, unaltered documents of the past. They require a supplement, an explanation, an expert opinion, an editorial point of view, which the surrounding restoration is there to provide: if the weathered stones appear framed by a partial replica of a Roman theater, then the visitor is gently predisposed to read them as ancient Roman stones. After a visit to Arles circa 1905, Sigurd Curman, Sweden's influential National Antiquarian, praised the "sensibly and instructively executed supplementary works which identify themselves clearly without spoiling the overall impression of the monument."[1]

The physical building material that makes up monuments can sometimes be an opaque document — difficult to read. Precisely this opacity legitimates the need for a contemporary supplement that will illuminate its meaning — document and supplement are mutually constitutive. But the supplement, by definition, needs to appear secondary to the document, even if without it the document cannot function as such. So contemporary architects pour a great deal of creative effort into making their work appear reversible and unobtrusive, even if, in the case of the Arles Theater, it would be physically impossible to separate the new stones from the ancient Roman ones without inflicting some degree of material damage to the latter.

Monumentaries are characterized by their dual nature as both documents and supplements, and by the tensions within the work that this duality creates at the aesthetic and conceptual levels. Monumentaries are works of architecture, but they defy some of our expectations of what architecture is. We are accustomed to appreciate architecture and artworks as objects that "hold together" as unified aesthetic experiences. But monumentaries often appear disaggregated aesthetically, with their supplements being only occasionally expressed. In other words, the supplement does not necessarily bring together the fragments of the original work under a unified aesthetic. In this sense monumentaries are close to documentaries, where the point of view of the director is (usually) only overtly introduced at key junctures in the film. Whereas a typical fiction film is completely subsumed in the aesthetic vision of the director, in a documentary the director must try both to reveal his or her creative license more obviously and to conceal it more cunningly. Directors of documentaries and architects of monumentaries have to overtly call attention to their hand in order to give the reassuring appearance that the rest of the film or building has not been tampered with and that therefore, on the whole, it can still qualify as evidence. The supplement, in other words, must be so highly visible, so incredibly obvious, as to be ignorable, something we can mentally remove from the work itself. The supplement in a monumentary functions like the stage in a play. Its obviousness is the enabling element for the necessary

Giorgio Grassi and Manuel
Portaceli, ancient Roman
theater in Sagunto, Spain

suspension of disbelief. This practice of making the supplement apparent
was canonized in the 1964 Venice Charter, which demanded that every
supplement to a monument "be distinct from the architectural composition
and must bear a contemporary stamp."[2]

### 3.

But how do we know if we are expressing a supplement too obviously
or too indistinctly? Let's look at an example that has been condemned for
being excessively obvious: the monumentary created by architects Giorgio
Grassi and Manuel Portaceli at the ancient Roman theater in Sagunto,
Spain. The ruins that remained in the 1970s were mainly the three tiers of
*cavea*, or semicircular rows of seating. The *scaenae frons*, or high enclosing
wall behind the stage, was entirely missing, save for the foundations.

Grassi and Portaceli wanted to create a monumentary that would
convey the original architectural experience of an ancient Roman theater.
They were designing in 1985, during the years of postmodernism, at the
height of the Italian school of typological urban morphology, which Grassi,
Gianfranco Caniggia, and Gian Luigi Maffei helped shape, and which Aldo
Rossi and Rafael Moneo disseminated internationally.[3] In order to express
the ideal of the Roman theater building type, Grassi and Portaceli thought
it essential to construct a new wall behind the stage as high as the
original *scaenae frons*. They were very careful to make it very obviously
contemporary, building it out of unadorned yellow brick to differentiate it
from the original grey stone. Following the standard archaeological
practice of anastelosis — a term initially describing the reerection of the
fallen stele around Greek temples — they inserted some remaining ancient
fragments into the new brick wall in order to give a sense of how highly
ornate the original *scaenae frons* would have been.

Despite the architects' attempt to follow convention and render the
supplement in an obvious fashion, the project was heavily criticized
immediately upon completion in 1993. Preservation architect Antonio
Almagro protested: "The contemporary spectator or visitor that enters the
space of the theater will find that, of the surfaces presented to his or her
sight, not even a fourth part are original Roman remains."[4] The supplement

seemed to him too obvious and too overwhelming of the original. It was so present that it could not be ignored or imagined away. Such was the uproar that the socialist municipality was taken to court by the opposing conservative party.

After decades, the Spanish Supreme Court decreed that the supplement had to be physically removed and the theater returned to its "original state."[5] Arguably, this original state was precisely what Grassi and Portaceli attempted to express in their project. But the Spanish Law of Cultural Patrimony forbids reconstructions in new materials, and only permits reconstructions based on the anastelosis of original fabric. Despite the supplement's clear appearance as something extrinsic to the work, it proved to be impossible to extricate from the ruins. In 2009, the Regional Supreme Court of Valencia argued it was physically, legally, and financially impossible for it to carry out the orders of the Spanish Supreme Court.[6] So the supplement still stands.

Almagro's emblematic critique further cues us to the paradoxical status of the supplement: it must be obviously expressed but also appear insubstantial, in both senses of the word, as a material that can be seen through and that is meaningless. This insight has led some creators of monumentaries to experiment with transparent materials, like glass and plastics. Architect Franco Minissi became well known for his transparent plastic supplements, especially his coverings of the *cavea* of the Greek Theater at Heraclea Minoa (Agrigento, 1960–63).[7] But the norm, as we've seen in Arles and Sagunto, is for supplements to be expressed with opaque materials. Using visual techniques such as "phenomenal transparency,"[8] opaque supplements can achieve disappearing effects by carefully matching the original's regulating lines while completing its missing volumes in order to create the sense of continuity, overlapping fields, depth, and so on. When taking in the monumentary as a whole, supplements appear as a material through which we can glean or imagine aspects of the original that are in fact not there.

#### 4.

Done properly, the supplement confounds, blurs the line between reality and fiction, and allows us to suspend disbelief, to satisfy our desire for meaning, to see what we want rather than what is before us: to experience the monumentary as unassailable documentary evidence of the past. The supplement plays on our human propensity towards binary thinking: its materiality is so overdetermined as something artificial and meaningless that it makes everything else around it, namely the original, appear authentic and deeply significant.

Monuments without supplements are rare, and for a reason. Recently, a municipal maintenance team discovered a rare unsupplemented six-thousand-year-old Celtic tomb in the Galician village of Ardesende, in northwestern Spain. They confused it with an old picnic table with broken benches, and with the best of intentions, demolished it and replaced it with a new table and benches, made of shiny new polished granite slabs to meet the standards of the most exacting picnicker.[9] The site had been documented by archaeologists and was officially listed as a Resource of Cultural Interest, but it was never supplemented. Similar cases abound of untreated monuments being misidentified as insignificant objects. In 2013, Belizean construction workers tore down a 2,300-year-old Mayan temple they mistook for a pile of rubble to make gravel for road filler.[10] Without a supplemental treatment, monuments can be unrecognized as such: invisible to the untrained eye.

Ambiguous legibility threatens the existence of monuments; in order to recognize something, we must by definition have seen it before. This means that it would be theoretically impossible for us to identify a construction we had never seen before as a monument. This is the primary role of supplements: to impose conventional attributes upon the extraordinary objects that will render them recognizable as monuments, that is, as evidentiary documents of the past.

#### 5.

Every discipline has its supplements, but only some have turned the supplement itself into their central endeavor and benchmark of creativity.

Erechtheion's caryatid column in the Acropolis Museum, Athens, Greece

The annals of preservation theory are filled with treatises and reflections on how to best express supplements. The same is not true in painting, for instance. Painting theory relegates supplements to the margin. The frames we put on paintings help to supplement them by establishing a clear inside and outside of representation. They draw the line between what we should attend to and what we should ignore, what is intrinsic and extrinsic to painting.

One could say, following Jacques Derrida, that the very idea of painting rests on the notion of the frame.[11] Derrida's philosophical analysis of the constitutive role of frames in paintings was all the more significant because art theorists had not seriously examined frames up to that point; in fact, they continue to mostly overlook them. Painters still don't design frames. It is worth mentioning, however, that at some point after World War II some painters realized that the frame — especially the wrong frame — could completely alter the reading of their work. They have since pushed to have their paintings hung frameless.

Derrida named the frame the *parergon* — from the Greek *para*, that which is next to the *ergon*, the work. "A *parergon* comes against, beside, and in addition to the *ergon*, the work done (*fait*), the fact (*le fait*), the work, but it does not fall to one side, it touches and cooperates within the operation, from a certain outside."[12] The *parergon* is a supplement to the existing work, a treatment that refashions it slightly, enhances it, and helps it achieve the presence and meaning it should have but cannot attain alone.

Derrida's description of the *parergon* doesn't fully capture the nature of the supplement in monumentaries. To be sure, monumentary supplements also refashion the work, physically and conceptually. Like the frame of a painting, monumentary supplements also *are* the work. They are also shot through with an ambiguous status: they might or might not be considered part of the work. Monumentary supplements also operate conceptually on the work from "a certain outside." But physically, they are part of the work and protect the work from further decay. In this sense their belonging to the work is not merely rhetorical. Monumentary supplements cannot be physically removed without letting the monument

Apergon on the southern wall of the Propylaea, Acropolis, Athens, Greece

incur significant damage, even total collapse. Monumentary supplements do not, as is often claimed, reconstruct the work. Rather, they obstruct it. The word "obstruct" shares the Latin verb *struere*, meaning to build, with construction; but it carries a different Latin prefix: *ob-*, meaning against. It is a buildup *against* the work that holds up the work, like the scaffolding against a wall.

As an obstruction, a monumentary's supplement delays our gratification, postpones conclusive meaning. But it does not deny it. It simply stands in the way of it, holds it in abeyance for a moment in the future anterior, when the monument will have been understood without supplements. The supplement therefore casts itself as a part of the work that must be removed in order to illuminate the work, to fully grasp it. In ancient Greek architecture, this part of the work was called the *apergon*. A building's blocks of ashlar were delivered to the construction site unfinished, with rough surfaces. These extra few centimeters were meant as a protective covering for the stone during transport and installation. Once the stone was safely installed, the *apergon* was struck from the stone as the surface was rendered and the architecture revealed. Perhaps the world's most famous *apergon* is the southern wall of the Propylaea, which was never removed because of the drain on Athenian coffers of the Peloponnesian War of 431 BCE. Starting especially in the Renaissance, the *apergon* was recognized as beautiful in itself and aestheticized as rustication on buildings of all sorts.

To recognize the monumentary supplement as the work's *apergon* is also to move beyond the tendency in preservation theory to analyze historic buildings according to false dichotomies that divide their fabric into parts: one being intrinsic original documentary evidence and the other cast as extrinsic, derivative, contemporary interpretation. It will bring us closer to grasping monumentaries for what they are rather than how we desire to see them; to appreciating the contemporary forms of expression alongside the pasts that they support and the futures they help fabulate, rather than continuing to insist on the traditional concept of the monument as an immutable relic of the past.

## Notes

An earlier version of this essay was published in *E-Flux* 66 (October 2015).

1    Sigurd Curman, "Principles of Restoration: Examples and Desiderata (1906)," *Future Anterior* 7, no. 2 (2010): 68.

2    ICOMOS, "International Charter for the Conservation and Restoration of Monuments and Sites (The Venice Charter, 1964)." http://www.icomos.org/charters/venice_e.pdf.

3    For a good primer on the school of typological urban morphology, see Gianfranco Caniggia and Gian Luigi Maffei, *Composizione architettonica e tipologia edilizia*: vol. 1, *Lettura dell'edilizia di base;* vol. 2, *Il progetto nell'edilizia di base* (Venice: Marsilio Editori, 1979).

4    Antonio Almagro, "Arde Sagunto: La Polémica Restauración del Teatro Romano," *Arquitectura Viva*, no. 32 (September–October 1993): 67. My translation.

5    Manuel Marín, "El TS echa abajo la rehabilitación del Teatro Romano de Sagunto: Considera que su reconstrucción vulnera la Ley de Patrimonio Histórico," in *Diario ABC* (October 18, 2000), 48.

6    "El TSJ considera 'imposible' demoler las obras del Teatro Romano de Sagunto," *El Mundo* (April 27, 2009), http://www.elmundo.es/elmundo/2009/04/24/valencia/1240574086.html.

7    Beatrice A. Vivio, "Transparent Restorations: How Franco Minissi Has Visually Connected Multiple Scales of Heritage," *Future Anterior* 11, no. 2 (Winter 2014): 1–17.

8    Colin Rowe and Robert Slutzsky, "Transparency: Literal and Phenomenal…," *Perspecta*, no. 8 (1963): 45–54.

9    Margarita Lázaro, "Denuncian la construcción de un merendero sobre un yacimiento arqueológico de más de 6.000 años," *El Huffington Post*, http://www.huffingtonpost.es/2015/08/24/yacimiento-arqueologico-merendero_n_8031478.html.

10    "Mayan pyramid bulldozed by Belize construction crew," BBC News (May 14, 2013), http://www.bbc.com/news/world-latin-america-22521669.

11    Jacques Derrida, *The Truth In Painting*, trans. Geoff Bennington and Ian McLeod (Chicago: University of Chicago Press, 1987).

12    Ibid., 45.

Jorge Otero-Pailos is an Associate Professor and rising Director of the Master of Science in Historic Preservation Program at Columbia University GSAPP.

# Obsolescence

## Daniel M. Abramson

In 1910, the landmark Gillender Building at the corner of Wall and Nassau streets fell to the wrecking ball. At its birth in 1897, it had been the world's loftiest office tower, but only thirteen years later, it was being rubbled for a taller, more up-to-date structure. Still physically sound, it was considered uneconomic and expendable, worthy only of destruction and replacement, in a word, obsolete.

The term *obsolescence* was first applied in English to the built environment to explain the demise of buildings like the Gillender brought low by "the influence of fashion, change of habit, competition, development of new territory and shifting of the centres of population and business," wrote New York engineer Reginald Pelham Bolton in 1911. "The useful or economic existence of all classes of buildings, in the rapid march of modern conditions, is constantly shortening."[1] With this New York vignette begins a history of obsolescence, eventually to gird the globe, wending its way through the twentieth century and into the present, offering lessons on managing change in a crowded terrain, a *tabula plena*.

After the Gillender Building's demise and Bolton's pioneering treatise, analysis of architectural obsolescence received further impetus with the introduction of the US corporate income tax in the 1910s, which included deductions for the cost of obsolescence. The National Association of Building Owners and Managers (NABOM) conducted membership surveys and "autopsies" of demolitions in its Chicago home, to understand the phenomenon and establish building life-span numbers for tax purposes. Publicized widely, NABOM's discourse resonated with American popular imagination, then witnessing an epidemic of building demolitions and a flood of expendable consumer goods. A 1935 bibliography listed some 125 entries on the subject.[2] "Blessed word," wrote the economist W. C. Clark, "which the income tax has forced upon our acquaintance and which we delight to roll upon our tongues because of its euphonious length and the impression of technical competence which its free use seems to convey."[3] Chaotic destruction was thus given a logic and a name — obsolescence — a process of seemingly inevitable innovation and supersession, producing economic development and progress.

In the following decades of the 1930s through the 1950s, the idea of architectural obsolescence was extended by urban planners to the scale of the city. In the US, urban obsolescence indicated a district's sub-standard economic, health, and infrastructure performance thus primed for demolition and renewal. In Europe, the term focused more on social factors, appropriate where the state rather than private investment often led development. "In both the Eastern and Western blocs," writes historian

Florian Urban, "obsolescence was the catchword of the time."[4] By the late 1950s the notion of built-environment obsolescence, in all its contexts, varieties, and scales — from capitalist to socialist, America to Europe, offices to cities — had become a dominant paradigm for comprehending and managing change. "The annual model, the disposable container, the throwaway city have become the norms," observed American preservationist James Marston Fitch.[5]

How did architects respond? At first by denial. In the 1920s and 1930s, traditionalists stuck to classical forms embodying permanence and durability. Even avant-gardists like Le Corbusier continued to seek "a sure and permanent home."[6] There were exceptions, of course. In Europe, the Czech shoe manufacturer Tomáš Baťa railed against "obsolete houses that will strangle and suffocate the next generation," and so projected twenty-year life spans for the factories and dwellings of his famed company town of Zlín.[7]

But it was not until the postwar years of prosperous consumerism that a younger generation of architects faced up to obsolescence's challenges. In the 1960s, University of London researchers produced in-depth studies discovering, for example, that hospital labs obsolesced faster than patient wards. From another angle, English architect Cedric Price promoted "an expendable aesthetic" and "planned obsolescence," characterizing some of his own designs, like the unbuilt Fun Palace, as "short-life toys."[8] In Japan, the Metabolist group extolled evanescent form-making: "There is no fixed form in the ever-developing world."[9]

But it was in design, not words, that architects engaged most deeply with obsolescence. The prime solution was the open-plan factory shed, widely adapted for schools and offices, hospitals and museums. Mies van der Rohe's New National Gallery in Berlin represented an apotheosis of the type: a perfect frame of infinite interior adaptability versus unforeseen change. Other architects, however, rejected the factory shed's monolithic exterior massing as too static for a dynamic age. Instead they promoted fluid, indeterminate design, like Northwick Park Hospital outside London (1961–76, Llewelyn Davies and Weeks), the largest British medical complex of its day, which featured a loose-jointed site plan of demolishable blocks and extendable ends, linked by a longer-lasting internal circulation spine. Permanence and impermanence harmonized in an age of obsolescence was the theme, too, of the megastructure, like Archigram member Peter Cook's Plug-In City project (1964–65), featuring a long-term, infrastructural latticework supporting plug-in components of shorter life cycles, from hotels to offices to shops. Megastructures and Plug-In City are not examples of *tabula rasa* utopianism, as sometimes supposed, but rather rational abstractions of *actually existing* urbanism: the modern city already filled with objects, obsolescing and replacing itself at different rates.

At the same time in the 1960s evolved an impassioned counter-reaction to obsolescence, which refused its logic of supersession and expendability. Concrete brutalism, for example, initiated by Le Corbusier's Unité d'Habitation, became a worldwide vernacular in the 1960s and 1970s, embodying permanence against obsolescence's flux. The renewal of traditional expression by Aldo Rossi, Louis Kahn, Robert Venturi, and others, launching postmodernism, revalued historical imagery. Preservationism also witnessed a dramatic upswing in the 1960s, becoming more populist around the globe, and incorporating recent and vernacular structures. Preservationism revalues objects otherwise destined for the discard pile with historical and affective meanings, reversing the logic of obsolescence, which conceived the passage of time as purely corrosive. Adaptive reuse and gentrification also gathered steam during this period, fueled by activists like Jane Jacobs, who rejected urban obsolescence's wholesale destruction of city districts. The profligate waste of obsolescence also offended 1960s environmentalism, which led to ecological architecture. Indeed, what we today call sustainability could be said to encompass *all* the counter-tactics to obsolescence that arose in the 1960s, from adaptive reuse to postmodernism to preservationism to ecological design, which prioritized the conservation rather than expendability of resources, both natural and human-made.

The richness of 1960s architectural culture precisely reflected the passions of a contest over obsolescence still hanging in the balance, the two sides equally creative and fervid. But by the early 1970s the matter

Tod Williams and Billie Tsien, Asia Society Hong Kong Center, Hong Kong, 2011

was largely settled, against designing for obsolescence. Financial constraint in the wake of oil crises dried up resources for replacement. Welfare state constriction eroded public patronage for renewal. Popular activism put an end to top-down bureaucratic planning. The grand dreams of a throwaway, expendable, plug-in future foundered on the shoals of economic, political, and cultural reversals. Instead, sustainability became the ruling paradigm. Notwithstanding some exceptions — Asian urban development and several building types (e.g., sports stadia and suburban teardowns) — the dominant ideology of sustainability — who argues against it? — now generally inclines public opinion towards adaptive reuse or some other form of preservation over knee-jerk demolition. UNESCO's World Heritage rubric continues its global march.

As such, obsolescence no longer drives design as it once did, when architects experimented imaginatively with factory sheds and indeterminacy, megastructures and plug-ins. Only occasionally does contemporary architecture grant creative significance to obsolescence. Rem Koolhaas is an exception. Trained in late-1960s London, Koolhaas retains that moment's romance with obsolescence, particularly in his admiration for Cedric Price: "He was a sceptic torturing a conservative discipline."[10] Koolhaas' unrealized plan for Paris's La Défense district (1991) "declared that every building in this entire zone that is less than twenty-five years [old] has to be destroyed."[11] In practice, Koolhaas expresses his understanding of obsolescence in smaller-scale details, as at the Illinois Institute of Technology campus center (1997–2003), whose elements look under construction, still provisional.

However marginalized, the history of obsolescence still has lessons to teach. Attend to the temporality of function, it suggests; the life of a building matters. Taking obsolescence seriously teaches the value of transcendence, too. We need to face buildings' mortality as we face our own. The history of obsolescence demonstrates the value as well in a vibrant architectural culture of the impulses both for extreme transformation and resistance to it. This was the characteristic struggle of the 1960s. Today the impulses stand imbalanced, sustainability in the ascendant, obsolescence eclipsed. In Hong Kong, at the recent Asia

Pavel Mudřík and
Pavel Míček,
Building No. 23
rehabilitation,
Zlín, Czech
Republic, 2006

Society Center building by Tod Williams Billie Tsien Architects, a new
steel-columned walkway runs at a respectful distance from the restored
massive masonry wall of an old explosives magazine berm. The past is
a precious jewel, set off from present and future.

Less refined but more instructive, and expressive of the lessons of
obsolescence, is the temporality of a renovated factory building in Zlín,
Czech Republic. Here, a century ago, the shoe manufacturer Tomáš Baťa
imagined twenty-year building life spans. But in 2006, the frame of
Building No. 23 was refurbished for a Business Innovation Center by Pavel
Mudřík and Pavel Míček. The building has also been augmented with
projecting bronze bays. But, more significant, something has been
subtracted from the architecture. To lighten the structure, broad voids
appear in the upper floors, shrinking the historical frame. Baťa's intention
— a limited-life architecture — is honored unconsciously. Building No. 23
in Zlín embodies preservation, growth, *and* attrition all at once, treating the
past flexibly, not reverentially. The past is visibly released. The present is
open, as is, implicitly, the future. In this design are lessons from the
age of obsolescence, showing how to deal with a crowded field radically
and imaginatively.

## Notes

1    Reginald Pelham Bolton, *Building for Profit: Principles Governing the Economic Improvement of Real Estate* (New York: De Vinne, 1911), 75, 68.

2    Mary Ethel Jameson, "Obsolescence in Buildings: A Selected List of References," in *Selected Readings in Real Estate Appraisal*, ed. A. N. Lockwood et al. ([January 1935] Chicago: American Institute of Real Estate Appraisers, 1953).

3    W. C. Clark, "Obsolescence," in *Property Management: Proceedings and Reports of the Property Management. Annals of Real Estate Practice*, vol. 5 (Chicago: National Association of Real Estate Boards, 1925), 143.

4    Florian Urban, *Neo-Historical East Berlin: Architecture and Urban Design in the German Democratic Republic 1970–1990* (Farnham: Ashgate, 2009), 44.

5    James Marston Fitch, *Historic Preservation: Curatorial Management of the Built World* (New York: McGraw-Hill, 1982), 31.

6    Le Corbusier, *Towards a New Architecture*, trans. Frederick Etchells (1931; New York: Dover, 1986), 263.

7    Daniel M. Abramson, "Obsolescence and the Fate of Zlín," in *A Utopia of Modernity: Zlín*, ed. Katrin Klingan (Berlin: JOVIS, 2009), 165–67.

8    Cedric Price, "Activity and Change," *Archigram* 2 (1962), n.p.; Cedric Price and Joan Littlewood, "The Fun Palace," *Drama Review: TDR* 12, no. 3 (Spring 1968): 129–30.

9    Noboru Kawazoe, "Material & Man," in Kiyonori Kikutake et al., *Metabolism: The Proposals for New Urbanism* (Tokyo: Bijutu Syuppan Sha, 1960), 48.

10    Rem Koolhaas, in conversation with Lynne Cooke, "Architecture and the Sixties: Still Radical after All These Years," *Tate Etc.* 2 (Autumn 2004), www.tate.org.uk/tateetc/issue2, accessed July 9, 2009.

11    Rem Koolhaas, "Urban Operations," *D: Columbia Documents of Architecture and Theory* 3 (1993): 53.

Daniel M. Abramson is an Associate Professor of Art History and Director of Architectural Studies at Tufts University.

# Governance

**Eduardo Rojas**

The practice of conserving urban heritage is well established and is making significant contributions to protecting the material capital inherited from previous generations. However, current approaches to urban heritage conservation exhibit a series of important constraints and shortcomings: they retain much of the "monument-and-its-surroundings" focus suggested in the Venice Charter (1964) and subsequent documents,[1] and are concerned with a limited set of sociocultural values of the heritage (mostly historic, aesthetic, and spiritual). Furthermore, they employ rigid conservation regulations requiring owners to maintain the properties as they were at the time conservationists consider appropriate; and they rely heavily on the government to finance the conservation effort. The restrictive regulations discourage private investment, and governments cannot conserve and maintain an ever-growing number of listed monuments.

The current approaches to conservation are turning urban heritage into a liability: a burden for the government and the city. One the one hand, governments are being forced to devote scarce public funds to the conservation of the heritage, and on the other, property owners are prevented from putting the properties to the highest and best use demanded by the real estate market. Not surprisingly, urban heritage conservation is hotly contested. It is promoted by only a handful of social actors in the city — mostly the cultural elite and scholars — while property owners and developers oppose it much of the time. Local communities often see few benefits in listing their neighborhoods and are either indifferent or mildly opposed. These conflicts oftentimes preclude the ability of urban sites, dense with architecture and public spaces, to adapt to the ever-changing demands of urban life.

This does not need to be the case — urban heritage can be an asset, for a wide range of private and public stakeholders. If put to good use while protecting its sociocultural values, urban heritage can be a resource for the social and economic development of its communities. This is the basic tenant of the conservation strategy based on the adaptive rehabilitation of heritage properties. When the material capital inherited by a city is adapted to satisfy contemporary needs with sustainable financing, it acquires an economic value. That is, urban heritage can, in addition to bringing sociocultural benefits to society, generate a flow of economic benefits.[2]

Unfortunately, real estate markets do not produce this outcome. In depressed heritage areas, development restrictions from conservation ordinances drive owners to under-invest in their properties. This disinvestment causes properties to decay and to be declared a nuisance, thereby facilitating their demolition and redevelopment. In heritage areas receiving development pressures, properties would be altered beyond their carrying capacity or demolished to generate the short-term profits sought by real estate developers. The government alone cannot compensate for this market failure. Faced with competing demands from multiple social needs — health, education, poverty alleviation, and public safety — governments at best undertake sporadic and limited interventions. Conservation regulations are difficult to supervise and are often ignored. This makes the conservation of the urban heritage unsustainable and fosters the loss of an accumulated material capital.

The conservation of the urban heritage must attract new social actors to use the heritage and contribute to its conservation, with a focus on uses that enhance the sociocultural values of buildings and public spaces. Neither public regulations nor free market development alone can produce the sustainable conservation of urban areas; instead, the process requires an intelligent balance of regulation and investment. The conservation effort needs structured cooperation between the government and the private sector and the combined use of instruments from heritage conservation and from urban rehabilitation. Coordinating public and private interventions means combining public guidelines for development and public support for infrastructure with the resources and market knowledge of private investors. To allow this cooperation, the heritage conservation discipline must contribute flexible regulations that adjust the level of conservation of buildings and public spaces according to their contribution to the sociocultural values of the heritage area. The urban rehabilitation discipline should provide instruments and interventions to bring new activities to abandoned and deteriorated heritage areas or to rebalance the uses in response to intense and conflicting development pressures. The materialization of the economic values of a heritage area then becomes instrumental in conserving its sociocultural values, turning the effort more sustainable.

Critical for the long-term sustainability of urban heritage conservation is to retain current users and attract new users and investors. This expands the range of social actors (stakeholders) committed to conservation, and attracts private resources for the adaptive rehabilitation of heritage properties. The current reduced set of stakeholders that commonly have a peripheral interest in urban heritage areas — the cultural elite, philanthropists, and government's cultural entities — needs to be replaced by a varied set of committed stakeholders that also includes households willing to live in the area, merchants, entrepreneurs and service providers finding it advantageous to do business there, and out-of-the-area customers and visitors. Their demand for rehabilitated space attracts investors and developers. This materializes the economic use values of the urban heritage. The heritage area must be as attractive as a place of living, working, visiting, and investing as other dynamic neighborhoods of the city, and not the preserve of tourists and schoolchildren on history tours. Conserving listed private buildings then becomes the users' responsibility. Governments can then focus on providing public infrastructure and services and mitigating the ill effects of gentrification.

The fruitful cooperation of public and private actors and the combined use of concepts and instruments of conservation and urban rehabilitation are difficult to attain under the existing governance mechanisms for the conservation of the urban heritage.[3] The structures of authority for conservation are defined by specialists, with little involvement from the community, and use strict regulations preventing most alterations to buildings and public spaces. The management of these structures of authority is usually delegated to public institutions or agencies in charge of culture that operate with little coordination with the city development plans and its institutions. The adaptive rehabilitation of urban heritage properties within their carrying capacity demands more flexible and participatory structures of authority implemented by institutions engaged in the integrated management of city development. They should ensure the fruitful cooperation among stakeholders, including public entities (public-public coordination), public and private actors (public-private cooperation), and private actors (private-private coordination).

Public-private coordination is needed to attract new stakeholders and private investment to urban heritage areas. Deteriorated or overcrowded historic neighborhoods are perceived as — and often are — too risky for real estate investors that fear that they will not be able to sell the rehabilitated space at the prices they expect and at the speed that is consistent with their expectations. Furthermore, property owners face a coordination dilemma. Even if they are interested in rehabilitating their properties, they are reluctant to be the first because they cannot compensate for the risk that the surrounding properties would not be rehabilitated. These problems can be addressed by private-public partnerships that can devise approaches to sharing the risks and benefits of the adaptive rehabilitation of properties. This is the main purpose of the mixed-capital urban rehabilitation corporations used in cities like Barcelona and Quito.

To attract and retain users and investors, the heritage area must offer high-quality infrastructure, public spaces, and urban services. This requires the coordinated efforts of many public agencies — mostly local, but also regional or national agencies, including public utilities often under private management. These agencies tend to focus on their sector agendas and have no incentives to synchronize their activities with others. Coordination committees or roundtables are insufficient, as their agreements are not binding. A widely used instrument for coordinating public entities is the "contract-plan." This is an instrument whereby an urban rehabilitation plan requiring contributions from all the public services is translated into a contract where the different agencies commit to implement the works they are responsible for within the time frame and the quality standard required by the plan. In most countries compliance with the contract is enforceable by law, thus ensuring the timely execution of the works.

Also important is the coordination of private investments in rehabilitation. A significant concern for investors in historic centers is the fate of the surrounding properties, which can enhance or diminish the value of their properties. A detailed conservation plan that is widely subscribed to by most stakeholders is a suitable instrument to reassure private investors. The plan specifies what can be done with each property to ensure that it retains the attributes that give it its heritage value. Thus investors know in advance what can they do to their properties and what their neighbors are allowed to do with theirs. This greatly reduces the uncertainty that is a major deterrent for investors.

Ensuring the fruitful cooperation of all the actors requires significant reforms to the governance of the urban heritage conservation process. It is necessary to shift focus from the monument and its surroundings to all the components of the urban structure that make up a heritage area: monuments, vernacular buildings, author architecture, public spaces, infrastructure, and urban services. The conservation process should rely on detailed but flexible regulations that modulate development restrictions of properties, adjusting to their contribution to the heritage value of the areas. Restrictions to development can range from complete conservation of significant monuments to contextual new construction in empty lots or containing irrecoverable ruins. The regulations need to be acceptable to the majority of interested parties, with a strong involvement of local stakeholders that are permanently invested in the area. The institutions enforcing these regulations must work in close association with the entities managing city development. The transparent management of the process, and effective accountability procedures, helps to reduce the conflicts of interest that emerge from the close relation between regulatory and development promotion entities.

Structural reforms of the institutions and regulations concerned with urban heritage conservation are profound but essential to transform these sites that are dense with buildings and public spaces, and charged with social and cultural meaning, into a resource for the social and economic development of cities. They pose significant challenges to the conservation profession, which can be understandably concerned with the scientific rigor of interventions that are driven by the energy of real estate markets. But they are feasible reforms — cities such as Cartagena in Colombia or Quito in Ecuador have implemented reforms consistent with what is suggested here while maintaining high standards of integrity and scientific rigor.

The new approach will not emerge as a result of a single administrative act; it requires a change in how the conservation effort is conducted and managed in historic centers. Well-conserved heritage areas can be as dynamic as any neighborhood in the city and require constant management to ensure the long-term conservation of their sociocultural values. This is a level of commitment that is not usual for conservation specialists, who in many cities tend to participate in "conservation programs" defined by the limited government resources available and tend to implement sporadic conservation works. When the conservation of the urban heritage becomes the concern of all social actors and turns heritage areas into dynamic sections of the city, the process requires permanent management, supervision, and stewardship. Urban heritage conservation then becomes an integral component of the management of the city and not an external imposition.

## Notes

1    For a complete compilation of the charters and related documents visit the ICOMOS Web site: http://www.icomos.org/en/

2    A complete discussion of this approach to the values of the heritage is in David Throsby, "Heritage Economics: A Conceptual Approach," in *The Economics of Uniqueness: Investing in Historic Cores and Cultural Heritage Assets for Sustainable Development*, ed. Guido Licciardi and Rana Amirtahmasebi (Washington DC: World Bank Publications, 2012), 45–73.

3    Stephen Bell indicates that "governance is about the use of institutions and structures of authority to allocate resources and coordinate and control activities in society." See Bell, *Economic Governance and Institutional Dynamics* (Melbourne: Oxford University Press, 2002), 1.

Eduardo Rojas is an independent consultant on urban development and a visiting lecturer in historic preservation at the University of Pennsylvania.

# Community

# Elizabeth Timme

The Frogtown neighborhood of Los Angeles is an area undergoing rapid cultural and spatial transformation. Framed by the intersection of freeways to the north, west, and south, and by the Los Angeles River to the east, Frogtown is an island of land with extremely limited vehicular access. Despite its isolation, the area is becoming an increasingly popular site for land acquisition, real estate speculation, and development projects. Directly adjacent to a section of the L.A. River that is slated to receive $1 billion plus dollars of federal and local investment, this neighborhood is facing an imminent shift in culture. My architecture and urban design practice LA-Más, which I founded in 2012 and now lead with my partner Helen Leung, is located in Frogtown. As an office, we became obsessed with leading the conversation on how the community could affect the impact of this demographic change. We sought to create an impartial process for gathering community input for an un-sanitized vision for neighborhood growth, authored by local residents and presented to developers. What this project also brought to light, however, were our limitations and biases as architects.

There is an unspoken tendency of those in positions of privilege and power to weight professional expertise over local interest. In the countless community meetings and discussions we organized in Frogtown, residents reiterated their preference to maintain the status quo, in contrast to our preconceived ideas about urban planning and transformation. While the local attachment to the existing made residents vulnerable to developers hawking images of contextualism, we struggled with our own biases to find ways of both enabling local interests and producing conditions of economic diversity and sustainability. Our involvement in Frogtown forced us to invent new models for negotiating with community interests, finding crossovers between the value of the existing and the advantages of growth and change.

We set out to involve ourselves centrally in the conversation surrounding investment and displacement. Because we were discussing what the future of the neighborhood would be if in the hands of the primarily Latino residents, we named this effort "Futuro de Frogtown." From talking to our neighbors and hosting barbeques and late night get-togethers, we were quickly wrapped up in the moral panic over perceived and real development pressures facing the community. After a few heated discussions, we decided to facilitate a conversation between the community at large and the large parcel owners, referred to as "the developers." What started out as a four-month process turned into ten months of intensive workshops, open houses and one-on-one meetings.

We partnered with a prominent developer to ground our conversations in the possible, and led six workshops to explore local opinions on the themes of: the nuances of community space, the ramifications of live/work and adaptive reuse, the design of manufacturing spaces, the complexities of affordable housing, the challenges of access and transportation, and lastly the future of the land use regulations.

In the beginning, we touted our ability as architects and planners to be the ideal facilitators. We were confident that we could use our combined arsenal of knowledge in land use and representational abilities to build local acuity in planning. Our goal was for the average community member, at the end of our engagement process, to be able to inform a piece of policy — which the city of Los Angeles was currently drafting to bridle development in the area. In the end, it became clear that the most essential ability in actualizing urban projects was not just the skills of analysis, representation, and design, but rather the faculty to negotiate between trained expertise and existing interests.

Although at face value what we were doing as community facilitators was, at least to us, quite straightforward, this project rapidly became enormously complex. What followed was an arduous, tense process of unpacking who we were as outsiders to the community, what our agenda was in hosting such a conversation, and what if any real impact our efforts to create a community-driven plan would have in the larger context of development citywide.

In the countless community meetings and discussions we organized in Frogtown, an area guaranteed to change, residents again and again reiterated their preference to maintain the status quo. While an understandable position, it was at odds with our learned values of urban planning, economic development, and sustainable growth. As we were drawn into the larger conversation between residents and developers, we also noticed various forms of manipulation by key stakeholders in places of power. Developers capitalized on the residents' fondness for the familiar by showing images that appeared contextual. We observed during design review presentations led by developers that when presented with urban alternatives, residents ignored all options other than what, on face value, would be most similar to existing conditions. When we pressed residents regarding what their larger values were when proposing a complete moratorium on development, we heard that the community wanted things to look the same, no matter what and at all costs. We informed residents that this would effectively displace the most vulnerable community members due to changes in the economy and development pressures.

There were major disadvantages to maintaining the status quo in this neighborhood. Providing no added housing for low-income residents when the city was in a period of historic housing shortages would threaten the diversity of the population of Frogtown. This concern was easily forgotten, however, when some of the residents of Frogtown showed images of the hastily designed, high-density projects slated to be built under the existing lax zoning policy. In addition, local architects in the community touted the exotic and unique character of the industrial fabric and advocated a complete halt to all projects that did not promote live/work or adaptive reuse. But these typologies of space did not fit the existing population and instead would support a new population with higher incomes, upward mobility, and flexible working conditions over the existing blue-collar resident who had traditionally lived in the area.

At this point, we still saw ourselves as neutral parties to a democratic and progressive process, which we were shaping organically in response to resident feedback and participation. We reiterated multiple times our lack of political goals apart from furthering community values. It was not until our project was nearly over that we realized what a mistake we had made in touting our neutrality. Because, of course, we were not neutral.

It is a fundamental desire to want to shape or guide one's environment. The community members in the neighborhoods where we work struggle to speak a shared language with designers, planners, and developers because they have not had the benefit of learning the ramifications of contextual issues and sustainable practices. Without an education in the potential of alternatives, a layperson will most often default into proposing the contextual and propagating the known.

There is an enormous amount of privilege that comes with being educated. Our office is composed of five core team members, all of whom have at minimum a master's degree in our respective fields of industrial design, community engagement, urban planning, public policy, and architecture. To have completed nearly a decade of study in multiple institutions of higher education does not make one impartial, just the opposite. Our team came to the table knowing what was best, not euphemistically but actually, from years of debate and study. However, what we realized is that we work in a highly charged political landscape that frames the cumbersome jurisdiction of a city that is a megalopolis. Knowing how to propose scalable systemic solutions for city growth and actuating projects with those same values are two different things.

To realize that our team had an agenda relative to our social status and cultural privilege was an incredibly hard thing to admit, let alone to write now. However, we had made our promises and we planned to keep them — we would promote the community's values with or without our educated, if privileged, agenda in our final report. In truth, we should have shifted our approach, retooled our workshops and promoted what we thought would support the community. We could have built an educational workshop process around explaining planning and policy from our clear political agenda. Instead, we dove in further and descended into the full depths of bias relative to those who would wish to halt all development.

Unfortunately, a policy which did not support sustainable growth for the community was adopted. In the end, Elysian Valley's proposed Q Condition ordinance was approved by the city council in November 2015, which down-zones the commercial and manufacturing parcels by reducing the buildable height to 30 feet and lot coverage to 60%, in addition to restricting residential use to live/work spaces only. Under these scenarios, 100% affordable housing developments are unlikely to be feasible. Housing demand will continue to rise while the feasibility of new housing projects diminishes, which may drive up prices and indirectly displace local residents in the adjacent residential area. The overall outcome of this policy change will result in physically appropriate projects that are misaligned with the social-economic diversity of the current community.

With traditional methods of affordable housing projects now untenable in the neighborhood, we began to unpack what we had learned from Futuro de Frogtown as part of a housing exhibit for the Architecture + Design Museum in the summer of 2015. We were at the crux of our own internal conflict — knowing what aspects of the built environment the community wanted to preserve, versus the types of policy recommendations that would support resident diversity in the long term. We began to develop an architecture and policy proposal that was in essence a manifestation of local community concern over "out-of-control development." We asked the question: How would housing growth in the neighborhood play out if all construction were resident-led and at a scale that was modest and contextual? What if it were literally in their backyard?

To make construction accessible and tenable to the average resident, we created a toolkit for building Accessory Dwelling Units (ADUs), the type of housing most congruous with backyard construction, and one that preserves the character of the neighborhood. By critically engaging lot-lines and speculative buildable space at the air-rights level, our strategy aims to reconsider the ADU (or "granny flat") as a new collective buildable area capable of supporting a diversity of renters. By pooling a neighborhood's existing untapped buildable space, residents may retain control — the chief concern voiced by community members throughout the engagement process.

We began this conversation by asking, "what is the true nature of resident-led development?" and our goal has been that the architectural product should serve as the basis for community engagement for the future of housing in the neighborhood. By facilitating a conversation between community and development, we dramatically departed from the traditional methods of accomplishing an urban planning or architectural project. Yet by that engagement, we ended up perceived not as facilitators, but harbingers of that change.

We assumed the fruits of our Futuro de Frogtown project would be a polite ten-page document outlining goals and policy recommendations to help educate future developers and inform developments in the neighborhood. That process, however, ended up further restricting the growth of the neighborhood at the hands of the most proactive and reactionary residents. Although we ultimately created an architectural project that fit somewhere in that oppositional context, the impression lingers that we did the community a disservice.

Of course, everyone is entitled to an opinion. However, an informed opinion is an arduous thing to achieve. Had we set out to change opinions rather than listen to and validate every one, we may have achieved a different outcome from our engagement process. And if our intent was to guide the growth of the neighborhood, that may have been our responsibility.

For us, Frogtown is a case study in the benefits and pitfalls of working in neighborhoods that have not historically been afforded the benefits or rights to growth. We entered this new community with every intention of wanting to have a more substantial conversation regarding development and gentrification, and what our role was in the space between those two market conditions. It wasn't until we accepted our own cultural bias as planners and architects that we were able to make progress in creating an alternative model for work beyond what we had known possible. But ultimately, the largest unintended consequence of Futuro de Frogtown was that our office was able to challenge our own educational model for engaging communities.

Elizabeth Timme is an architect and community advocate. She is co-founder and Co-Executive Director of LA-Más.

# Abstinence

## Ippolito Pestellini Laparelli

We live in a moment of extreme fascination with the past.

In his book *Retromania: Pop Culture's Addiction to Its Own Past*, music critic Simon Reynolds investigates the fixation of the music industry with going retro, through remakes, sequels, reenactments, mash-ups, and so on. He argues that there has never been "a society so obsessed with the cultural artifacts of its immediate past" and that generally, the current moment is one of cultural reminiscence. "Is nostalgia stopping our culture's ability to surge forward, or are we nostalgic precisely because our culture has stopped moving forward and so we inevitably look back to more momentous and dynamic times?" By extension, the same phenomenon seems to permeate all aspects of western cultural production, from contemporary art to cinema, fashion, product design, etc., and obviously also architecture.

The implications of a nostalgic surrender to the past as opposed to a proactive relationship with history are deep. Svetlana Boym investigates this opposition in *The Future of Nostalgia*: "At first glance, nostalgia is a longing for a place, but actually it is a yearning for a different time — the time of our childhood, the slower rhythms of our dreams. In a broader sense, nostalgia is a rebellion against the modern idea of time, the time of history and progress."[1]

The consequences for our practice of an increasing but nostalgic attention to the past are huge and potentially devastating: a growing resistance in accepting change and modernization as an inevitable evolution; philological restorations focused on a literal reconstruction of the past; preemptive norms forcing new projects to look like old ones, generating an undefined soup of past and present "authenticities."

At the Venice Architectural Biennale of 2010, our office, OMA, presented a body of work focused on our persistent preoccupation with preservation and with the past. The exhibition was symbolically named Cronocaos. It had the ambition to revitalize among architects the debate around preservation as a global and contradictory phenomenon with untheorized implications for architecture and beyond.

The exhibition showed the recent but exponential increase of scale and action of the "global task force of preservation to rescue larger and larger portions of our planet";[2] the inability of the current moment to negotiate the coexistence of radical change and radical stasis; the absence of tools in the arsenal of preservation to deal with and manage its effects, or how to keep the past "alive"; our growing fascination with the past and the "authentic," not as a historical and objective category, but rather a nostalgic, reengineered version of it; preservation's preference towards certain authenticities as opposed to politically uncomfortable ones, which are terminated even if historically relevant; the political implications of preservation as a tool for economic development, subject to political correctness more than to cultural concerns; the focus on preserving the exceptional and the lack of ideas for preserving the generic; the possibility of demolition as a necessary and opposite theory to preservation...

In tandem with our theoretical speculations, the exhibition also featured twenty-seven OMA projects that were never "presented before as a body of work concerned with time and history."[3] Spanning across more than thirty years of practice, they showed OMA's latent yet undeclared interest in preservation, highlighting twenty-seven architectural concepts of how OMA dealt with the existing, in different historical, cultural, and environmental contexts around the world.

Far from declaring any dogma, Cronocaos had the ambition to raise questions, highlighting contradictions and patterns, while implicitly recognizing the impossibility of a global single theory for preservation.

It is not a coincidence that Cronocaos happened at the climax of our theoretical interest in the subject and of our active involvement in practice through three key and very different projects, started more or less at the same time: Fondazione Prada in Milan, Il Fondaco dei Tedeschi in Venice, and the Garage Center for Contemporary Art in Moscow.

In Milan, Fondazione Prada occupies the spaces of a former nineteenth-century distillery. Crafted as a catalogue of curatorial techniques and display strategies, the project is conceived as a rich repertoire of spaces for the arts, ranging in scale and character. Three simple new architectural interventions were added to the existing structures to complement the catalogue of museum spaces: a large open-plan museum hall with a long beam gallery space on top, and a tower of stacked floors with incrementally increasing heights. Almost invisible from the outside, the project works as a continuous sequence of indoor/outdoor spaces, where old and new meet dynamically, hanging in balance in a state of permanent interaction. Two conditions that are usually kept separate here confront each other, offering an ensemble of fragments that will not congeal into a single image, or allow any part to dominate the others. While walking through the new complex, you are confronted with a collection of preservation techniques — from bare re-functionalization to the careful introduction of new volumes, from a verbatim reconstruction of a demolished building to the simple application of one layer of coating to inject new life into the preexisting. Far from any fetishist attachment to the existing, old and new seamlessly work together and sometimes are actually merged, to the point that one cannot say that Fondazione is either a preservation project or a new architecture, but rather a curated continuum of both.

In Venice, we faced the challenge of transforming a former sixteenth-century German trading warehouse (which became an eighteenth-century customs office, then a 1930s post office) into a contemporary department store. Almost entirely reconstructed with modern concrete technology during the fascist regime, the Fondaco dei Tedeschi is a historical palimpsest of modern substance, its preservation spanning five centuries of construction techniques. Regardless of the history of its adaptations and the objective lack of authenticity of its structure, its legal status of "monument" places it today under a severe regime of preservation, forbidding almost any change. Dealing with it meant facing this paradox. After years of creative negotiation with the city authorities, national heritage institutions, and local groups of defensive citizens, the project is now materializing. It is based on a finite number of local interventions and vertical distribution devices culminating in a new roof terrace space. Each intervention is conceived as a brutal excavation through the existing mass, liberating new perspectives and unveiling the real substance of the building to its visitors. With an almost forensic attitude, each new component serves as a way to show the stratification of materials and construction techniques. The preservation of the Fondaco dei Tedeschi is the history of its change: it avoids nostalgic reconstructions of the past and demystifies the "sacred" image of the historical building, revealing its authentic brutality.

In Moscow, the transformation of a soviet café into a contemporary art museum has offered the opportunity to experiment on the preservation of a generic modernist building. The original structure has been intentionally left bruised and repaired with minimal intervention, unveiling original tiles, brickworks, mosaics, and the generosity of Soviet architecture. The focus here is the preservation of the history of the building, and decay as part of that history; the new façade — translucent layers of polycarbonate panels containing all technical arteries — acts as an intelligent shrine around a concrete ruin. Similar to cases of "unintentional preservation" — ruins of Pompeii after the eruption of Vesuvius, abandoned Chernobyl or Fukushima after the nuclear accidents — at Garage, we preserved the found condition, keeping the existing building as an artifact, and added new elements to make it perform as a contemporary museum space. There is no "political" selection of what to preserve, but rather the intention to freeze a moment in history.

It might seem strange for a big architectural office to develop an obsession with preservation. Normally challenged by the expectations — and the burden — of delivering the next exceptional building, the idea to shift the focus to a more subtle understanding of context and to a more delicate presence is a big release.

Less obsessed with the need to affect the skyline of cities, the attention to preservation and more generally to the reuse of existing urban fabrics challenges architects with a different set of questions which are less focused on form and more on program, histories, systems, technology, materials, etc. The implication is simple: a radical shift from the egocentric and iconic to the invisible and contextual.

By doing this, preservation is a political act. It triggers city planners, developers, architects, and contractors to consider alternative models of operations, investing in the future of cities from their own past, reusing existing buildings as opposed to building new ones. Preservation can be an equally if not more efficient form of urban modernization and growth, avoiding inconsiderate accumulations of new buildings, subject to the fluctuations of the modern market and often left vacant before even coming into life.

In its ultimate manifestation and when the situation requires it, preservation can even shake the foundations of architectural practice, introducing the possibility of abstinence in the architect's repertoire. Doing nothing or almost nothing, avoiding designing and construction: these are powerful tools as much as their opposites.

### Notes

1    Svetlana Boym, *The Future of Nostalgia*
(New York: Basic Books, 2001), xv.
2    OMA, Cronocaos exhibition text, 12th
Venice Architecture Biennale, 2010.
3    Ibid.

Ippolito Pestellini Laparelli is an architect and partner at OMA.

# Diversity

## Interview with Winy Maas

**Bryony Roberts:** I'd like to ask you a few questions about how your practice, MVRDV, approaches reuse projects — how you see these projects differently than new construction projects, and how your strategies might compare with those of other practices today.

In terms of the analytical framework, I'm interested to know how you analyze historical architecture. How do you determine its value, both quantitative and qualitative, to contemporary cities, as a way to begin the design process?

**Winy Maas:** Well, obviously there is the economic assessment of an existing building, and also the ecological one. The ecological value, especially now in the days of the climate summits, is a highly accepted one. But the other issue is diversity. I still, maybe naively, dream about a kind of "biodiversity of architectures" over the planet. Maybe I'm one of the few people that wants to protest against complete generic-ness. So that's a question for me. Why biodiversity? Or why diversity? Does it have a social value in the end? Does it create communities that identify themselves with certain kinds of architectural appearances? Are there activities that are possible with a diversity of architecture?

**Bryony:** That's an interesting framework for looking at existing architecture, this question of diversity. How do you see the role of the architect in preserving or producing diversity?

**Winy:** Well to start with, I'm not against reusing. But I do doubt whether all new design needs can be fit into existing buildings. There is a new generation speaking out loudly, saying, "Oh, we can do it in the existing." But in quite a lot of cases, the new needs simply do not fit.

We have to ask — when do we allow for adaptation? And why? And how much? Do we adapt ourselves? Or do we adapt the built environment? Personally, I am more fascinated with the second direction, to adapt our environments to our future needs, rather than sticking to the old and reducing our imaginations.

Especially in the Third World, the message that we can fit everything in the existing is really problematic. If I am in Nairobi and I bring that message to some of the areas, the slum areas, it would never work. So there's a stupidity also in the reliance on reuse that needs to be nuanced.

**Bryony:** It's also interesting how you're dealing with a lot of ordinary, everyday building types in reuse projects, such as the recent Teletech campus in Dijon. To deal with a building that was so recent, from 2004, that had to be adapted, also seems to be a latent critique of typical preservation practices. It's moving away from a more monumental focus in preservation. Was that an intention with that project?

**Winy:** Yeah, partly. I doubt whether monumentality should be only reserved for the nineteenth century. Maybe after the nineteenth century there are already some series of elements to be monumentalized and/or reused.

But again, to be contradictory, I also question if we still need certain typologies. How many generic buildings do we need?

**Bryony:** Do you think current preservation guidelines, for example from UNESCO, should adjust in order to accommodate this more critical approach to conservation?

**Winy:** Well, within the preservationists there are already different groups. On the one hand you have the die-hard defenders, who are only interested in complete preservation without adaptation. Often they are from a generation that was confronted with erasure more than with preservation. But maybe now we see a new generation that is more nuanced in this matter and that wants to open itself up.

Although I do find certain elements of complete preservation interesting. When we love a certain building or a certain neighborhood, then it's also fine to protect it, as in a museum. But I find it intriguing to ask, where do you draw the line?

One city dealing with this is St. Petersburg, where they have so many monuments that they cannot afford to repair them all. So one approach is to turn it into a ruin, like Pompeii. Or secondly, you generate so much money just in the vicinity of these buildings that you can repair them by proximity. If, for example, you create a denser variance around the perimeter, then you can make a kind of wall around the old city. It gives it a distinct, protective character. That fascinates me, this kind of treatment.

While talking with you about it, I'm also starting to wonder how to work on this at the scale of the planet. How much do we owe in terms of our heritage? Where does it end? It could be useful to develop a kind of a catalogue of both the frontiers and our expansions.

**Bryony:** Yes, on that note, has your office seen a shift towards research topics that are more related to preservation? Or do you see any new frontiers for analysis that are important to look at, relative to this?

**Winy:** One research that we are doing at the moment is about how to adapt our façades, floors, and roofs — so basically the existing building —

with vegetable matter and with animal life. That fascinates me. So that research will come out soon, when we show different products through their value in the energy chain to attract animals. That's the diversity book that will come out, in about a half a year from now.

The beauty of it is when you see, say the Amsterdam canals, which are UNESCO monuments, with a kind of green touch everywhere. I think it's a sublime update on the old and it's kind of a hilarious provocation to allow not only birds to live there, but also animals. So that has a beauty in itself.

**Bryony:** That sounds incredible. Those kinds of schemes — I mean the really visionary ideas for reuse and transformation — do you think they necessitate a larger government involvement in planning? Or do you see these things as possible through public/private partnerships?

**Winy:** Of course I would love that! We develop visions and scenarios and our research is a little bit provocative, so it doesn't concentrate yet on that kind of implication. In a way we provide ideas that then other researchers are taking over, getting much bigger grants and much bigger value out of that. So I completely agree with you, that we should incorporate the possibilities of application and the market value of these kinds of ideas.

**Bryony:** Do you have a yearning in general for urban transformation being tied to government involvement and support? Or do you see visionary changes possible?

**Winy:** Well, that is another question.

**Bryony:** Yes, it is a different question!

**Winy:** And it's true that it is a subject that fascinates me. Can we do something which is bigger than only the building? And can it turn into urbanism in that respect?

One could say there is a kind of fashion of bottom-up projects, and, okay, fair enough. But is that covering everything? Can we manage with that? Can we achieve our energy systems? Can we allow for inclusion instead of exclusion? Bottom-up has a tendency to exclude, to keep it only for a specific community and specific group.

So these are subjects that fascinate me, to see how and when governmental forces are needed, or how to mobilize them under certain kinds of conditions. So yes, of course we collaborate with the politicians and actually with everybody. I mean, I always say, if 70% of the population hates our building, then we should not build it.

**Bryony:** These issues all came up very clearly with the project in Oslo for the new government quarter, the Nytt Regjeringskvartal, which we were both involved in. It was a particularly challenging interaction between architects, citizens, and government because of the controversies around heritage and preservation. Did you come away from that process with any useful lessons about dealing with government and heritage issues?

**Winy:** I liked the process as it was designed in the beginning, where people were asked to give deep reflections on how to deal with both heritage and architecture that represents government. So we took it on board in our first proposal by asking, what is the best symbol that we can do and how to choose? And we suggested a referendum between the different schemes.

I was equally fascinated by the raw reaction of the committee, saying, "No, you can't do that. You have to choose yourself." So, okay, then we just did what we wanted to do, and showed that. So the process in itself was intriguing. It was quite intellectual.

**Bryony:** Well, I think your proposal was courageous in its boldness. It was almost at the scale of a Superstudio project. You proposed this enormous wall around the government quarter, which framed the existing buildings. But in walling it off, it was creating both a government enclave and almost a building museum. So could you speak about why you went for such an extreme, provocative proposal? And how it was intending to frame history in a larger sense?

**Winy:** The funny thing is that you mentioned "provocative," which for me is the most modest proposal that we could imagine! But that's maybe almost provocative in its way.

**Bryony:** Ha, you mean because it was doing as little as possible on the site?

**Winy:** Yes. Well, I must say it could have been even more invisible, if we would have ducked the program. So under a certain kind of situation this was the most limited and most modest that was possible. I suppose it could have been even more modest — we could have buried the new ministries underground.

**Bryony:** I'm curious because we have a couple of people in the book who talk about the radicality of doing very little, or of doing nothing. Architects, you know, are sort of addicted to producing new objects. That can often be a very good thing, but it can be sometimes very interesting and challenging to try to do less. Is that something that you're working on? Or was that just a one-time exploration?

**Winy:** No. Of course, there is an entire Swiss generation specializing in that, in modesty. The whole Swiss architecture movement is completely drenched with modesty, so I would not say that modesty should be everywhere. I don't believe in that.

I think it is much more interesting to show courage. What can buildings do? Sometimes they have to be subtle, in preservation areas even more than in other places. But sometimes they have to behave boldly in order to activate revitalization.

We are discussing within our office how modest should we be, or how pronounced we should be. The whole strategic component of a building is one of the most interesting parts about the picture. The strategic aspect turns architecture into urbanism and makes it into a phenomenon beyond just an object.

**Bryony:** It seems like this problem of reuse will become only more pressing as we keep accumulating existing buildings. Do you see your practice taking on more and more of that work?

**Winy:** It's definitely not the only part. But I would say that whatever you build, you have to deal with the existing. Even if I make a building in a landscape, or in the sea, then I have to deal with the environmental constraints, and then I am always contextual in how I deal with the existing. In some cases it is not an existing building; it's existing landscapes.

The education of landscape architecture, which I had, makes this issue particularly explicit. It is much more inherent in the landscape approach than in architecture, because of the scale and the size of the operations. So in terms of responding to the context, if you include landscape, then we do it always.

Winy Maas is one of the founding directors of the architecture and urban planning firm MVRDV.

# Authorship

## Salvador Muñoz Viñas

Roland Barthes published "The Death of the Author" in 1967.[1] As the years passed, this brief essay became increasingly well known, and has now become the French philosopher's most frequently quoted paper. If only because of its ability to engage other thinkers in a fruitful discussion, it deserves a prominent place in the history of artistic thinking.[2]

In "The Death of the Author," Barthes stated that "the image of literature to be found in ordinary culture is tyrannically centred on the author,"[3] and called it a "historical fact" that the figure of the Author was "diminishing like a figurine at the far end of the literary stage."[4] For Barthes, the author was an unwarranted source of *authority* — and in fact he preferred to use the term "writer" or "scriptor." In doing so, Barthes was linking the "death of the author" to a sort of *revolutionary* liberation:

...Literature (it would be better from now on to say *writing*), by refusing to assign a "secret," an ultimate meaning, to the text (and to the world as text), liberates what may be called an anti-theological activity, an activity that is truly revolutionary since to refuse to fix meaning is, in the end, to refuse God and his hypostases — reason, science, law.[5]

Aside from these political overtones, Barthes was emphasizing the role of the receiver of the message in the process of the literary experience, and, by extension, that of any artistic experience. Indeed, his argument was not so different from what Wimsatt and Beardsley had already argued in 1946,[6] even though Barthes was stressing not just the interpersonal nature of the artistic experience, but rather, and more properly, its purely social nature. Barthes was arguing against the idea that the author is the only relevant factor in the artistic process. In his words:

The author is a modern figure, a product of our society insofar as, emerging from the Middle Ages with English empiricism, French rationalism and the personal faith of the Reformation, it discovered the prestige of the individual, of, as it is more nobly put, the "human person." It is thus logical that in literature it should be this positivism, the epitome and culmination of capitalist ideology, which has attached the greatest importance to the "person" of the author.[7]

Since its publication, "The Death of the Author" has become a widespread notion: when the term "death of the author" is mentioned, Barthes' essay is what first comes to most people's mind, as has likely been the case of the reader of this paper.

In this modest paper I do not aim to replace or challenge Barthes' original "death of the author," but rather to recall it to suggest that, in the field of heritage conservation, another less conspicuous "death of the author" might have played an important role in shaping this fascinating discipline. This "death of the author" is the death of the author who works in heritage conservation — the death of the author within the conservator.

It might be argued that conservators are not *authors* at all, but such an argument only reflects the fact that the *death of the author* has already been assumed in contemporary conservation thinking. In the beginning of conservation as we know it, the role of the the conservator as an *author* was openly acknowledged. Viollet-le-Duc stated that for the conservation architect, "there are always ways to reconcile his role as a conservator and as an artist" ("*il a toujours les facilités de concilier son rôle de restaurateur avec ce lui d'artist*").[8] In fact, for Viollet-le-Duc, the task of the conservator does not imply *abandoning* authorship, but rather *becoming* the author:

> The best option is to put oneself in the place of the original architect, and to guess what he would have done if he were back in the world and facing the same tasks assigned to us. (*Le mieux est de se mettre à la place de l'architecte primitif, et de supposer ce qu'il ferait, si, revenant au monde, on lui posait les programmes qui nous sont posés à nous-mêmes.*)[9]

Viollet-le-Duc published these words in 1849. A few decades later, however, things had changed in a substantial way. In 1893, Camillo Boito published his *Questioni prattiche delle belle arti*, in which he boldly argued against Viollet-le-Duc. For Boito, the object should show the imprints of its own, true history; therefore, any addition from the conservator would hinder its correct reading. Therefore, conservators should interfere as little as possible to the work they were dealing with, and if an addition was considered necessary, it should be easily recognizable. The conservator should not allow his own views, tastes, and preferences to play any role in the decision-making process: personal, private emotions were an ever-present danger, something that needed to be avoided at all costs. The conservator could be all too personal — all too human:

> The spirit of the conservator is human: he falls in love with the object of his own thoughts and faces the risk of going too far, aiming at perfection (*L'animo del restauratore è un animo umano: s'innamora*

*dell'oggetto de' propri pensieri e rischia di esagerare, intendendo alla perfezione).*[10]

For Boito, and for most conservation thinkers and practitioners after him, the role of the author (of his or her subjective tastes, biases, and creative abilities) had to be restrained as much as possible. In other words, the conservator should never aim at being an author, but rather something different, something neutral: a conservator as we know it. In fact, Boito considered it "a duty" (*un dovere*) to establish some kind of surveillance that would prevent the conservator's judgment from being "misled with pride" or "inflamed with passion."[11]

Boito's dismissal of human emotions is very much in line with Barthes' death of the author, for whom these emotions are an inherent feature of *the author*: "succeeding the Author, the writer no longer contains within himself passions, humors, sentiments, impressions."[12]

It could thus be said that the *author* within the conservator died in the late nineteenth century: it was killed by Boito, and then duly buried by Beltrami, Dehio, Giovannoni, and other conservation thinkers. For these theorists, conservation and authorship were to be seen as absolute opposites. In conservation, any temptation to authorship should be rejected.

If applied to conservation, Boito's and Barthes' *deaths of the author* are somehow similar, as both of them reject *authorship*. And yet, both of them are very different in nature: Boito's rejection of authorship in conservation was done in order to prevent authorship from hindering the correct reading of an object, while Barthes was rejecting the very existence of a "correct" reading. This is a crucial difference. These deaths are not just two instances of the same death: though both of them lead to the same place (the grave of the Author), they do so by walking opposite paths.

Barthes' *Death of the Author*, however, has a theoretical problem. It is indeed a beautiful idea, but, when applied to conservation, it may lead to a kind of theoretical nihilism. If no correct reading of a work exists, then why should conservators refrain from modifying the work at will? In fact, if no correct reading exists, why should conservation exist at all?

A good answer to this problem is perhaps that coming from what has been called "contemporary theory of conservation."[13] Many heritage theorists could agree with Barthes that no purely correct reading exists; however, for these theorists, it does not mean that all readings are equally valid. Indeed, some meanings of the work are more valuable than others, for more people, for a longer time. It is evident that the more valuable those meanings, the better. In this case, the conservator, too, should relinquish his passions, tastes, and feelings: he should die for the sake of providing the most valuable overall meaning.

In doing so, the conservator would no longer be bound by Boito's mandate to preserve all of the imprints of the history of the object. Indeed, for contemporary thinkers, some of these imprints may be more valuable than others, and eradicating some of them, or even all of them, may be the right thing to do in order to preserve or increase the overall, long-term value of the object.

This *death of the author* is less convenient than Boito's (which provides strict guidelines urging the preservation of all of the imprints of the history) or Barthes' (which provides no guidelines whatsoever). It requires careful assessment of the many values of the object, painstaking negotiation with all involved parties, and difficult decisions in order to gain the maximum benefit from the treatment. This may be complex and challenging, since the variety of values an object may embody (religious, economic, idelological, identitarian, sentimental, etc.) is endless: in some circumstances, a scientific reading may need to be privileged, while in others the main goal of the treatment may be turning the object into a better artwork — or allowing it to better symbolize a national identity, or making it better convey a religious idea, etc. In all cases, however, the author within the conservator needs to die in order to fulfill the needs, preferences, and expectations of those for whom conservation is done.

It takes courage.

## Notes

1   Roland Barthes, "The Death of the Author," *Aspen: The Magazine in a Box*, no. 5+6 (1967). *Aspen: The Magazine in a Box* had a quite restricted circulation. Most quotes from "The Death of the Author," including those in this paper, are taken from Roland Barthes, *Image Music Text: Essays Selected and Translated by Stephen Heath* (London: Fontana Press, 1977), 142–49.

2   An account of the inception and reception of the essay can be found in John Logie, "The Birth of 'The Death of the Author,'" *College English* 75, no. 5 (2013), 493–512.

3   Barthes, "Death of the Author," 143.

4   Ibid., 145.

5   Ibid., 147.

6   W. K. Wimsatt and M. C. Beardsley, "The Intentional Fallacy," *Sewanee Review* 54 (1946), 468–88.

7   Barthes, "Death of the Author," 142–43.

8   Eugéne Viollet-le-Duc, "Restauration," in *Dictionnaire raissoné de l'architecture française du XIe au XVIe siècle: Tome huitième* (Paris: Librairies-Imprimeries Réunies, 1849), 31. My translation.

9   Ibid., 32.

10   "...surveillance is a duty, given that the judgment of the watchman is not easily inflamed by passion or misled by pride." (*...la vigilanza e un dovere, se si considera che il giudizio di chi sorveglia non si lascia facilmente accendere dalla passione o fuorviare dall'amor proprio.*) Camillo Boito, *Questioni prattiche delle belle arti* (Milan: Ulrico Hoepli, 1893), 393. My translation.

11   Ibid.

12   Barthes, "Death of the Author," 143.

13   "By 'contemporary' we mean those ideas about conservation that have been developed since the 1980s. It might be argued that this is an arbitrary date, and that several earlier examples of 'contemporary' conservation thinking do exist. However, these are exceptions, and so the 1980s must still be considered to be quite representative." Salvador Muñoz Viñas, *Contemporary Theory of Conservation* (Oxford: Butterworth-Heinemann, 2005), xi–xii.

Salvador Muñoz Viñas is a Professor and the Director of the Conservation and Restoration of Cultural Heritage Department in the Polytechnic University of Valencia (UPV).

# Boredom

## Christian Parreno

With pejorative connotations in contemporary culture, preservation is often referred to as "the taxidermy of architecture." For instance, in April 2014, *The New York Times* wrote that although there is no "harm" in dismantling and potentially reassembling somewhere else the façade of the American Folk Art Museum, as part of the extension plans of MoMA, the act should not be mistaken as a "gesture for actual preservation" since "it's more like taxidermy."[1] Similarly, in April 2007 the *Chicago Tribune* exemplified "architectural taxidermy" with the redevelopment of the Farwell Building, in which the exterior was removed, cleaned, and restored before being reapplied to a new structure.[2] In both accounts, "the art of preparing and preserving the skins of animals, and of stuffing and mounting them so as to present the appearance, attitude, etc., of the living animal"[3] is transposed, in its most literal form, to architecture, turning preservation into "the artistic practice of arranging the façades of buildings so as to reenact their primary conditions." The irony of "preservation as taxidermy" derives not only from its anachronism but also from the impossibility of recuperating a lost moment in the life of an object. In the first case, the current efforts of architectural preservation are likened to the investigative and representational aims of a practice considered simultaneously artistic and precise in the nineteenth and early twentieth centuries. In the second, the assumption that architectural structures pass their prime and can become extinct questions the selection criteria of why some pieces of the built environment are enlivened and others are not. Additionally, the preoccupation with the façade as the skin of architecture exposes the essence of preservation as public and civic, implying that interventions that prolong the existence of buildings — or spatial conditions — require the acknowledgment of those who encounter them.

In "Teddy Bear Patriarchy: Taxidermy in the Garden of Eden, New York City, 1908–1936" (1984), Donna Haraway delineates preservation as a non-neutral endeavor, underpinned by gender and racial ideologies. The philosopher reconstructs the history behind the animals of the African Hall in the American Museum of Natural History, across from the heart of Central Park. According to the Museum, the exhibition — opened in 1936 — features a central composition of "a freestanding group of eight elephants, poised as if to charge, surrounded by 28 habitat dioramas ... with animals set in a specific location, cast in the light of a particular time of day."[4] The work is credited to Carl Akeley (1864–1926), "the naturalist, explorer, photographer, sculptor, and taxidermist who first conceived of this hall in 1909 and collected many of the specimens for it."[5] However,

"Teddy Bear Patriarchy" denounces the official account as a construction of "white and male supremacist monopoly capitalism,"[6] arguing that the work was actually performed by women — Akeley's two wives, Delia J. and Mary L. Jobe — and anonymous Africans who were recruited as labor. Through the assembly of evidence — some of it jealously guarded by the archive officers of the Museum[7] — the new history exposes preservation as a mechanism of power concerned with the extension and fortification of the hegemony of the past and its political structures. For Haraway, the attempt to control time through hunting and taxidermy is not only a confrontation to the female capacity of giving birth but also a teleological anxiety, proper of the modern belief that existential meaning can be conquered in a lifetime — "in immediate vision of the origin, perhaps the future can be fixed. By saving the beginnings, the end can be achieved and the present can be transcended."[8]

### Inadvertently Complicit with Power

Akeley did not intend to craft "a history of race, sex, and class in New York City that reached to Nairobi."[9] But retrospectively, according to Haraway, the design and construction of the African Hall expose preservation as an activity embedded in capitalism and personal interests. As an economic venture, Akeley's expeditions, hunting, and taxidermic experimentations — financed by the trustees of the Museum, including Kermit Roosevelt, J.P. Morgan, William K. Vanderbilt, and John D. Rockefeller III[10] — appear analogous to the selection in architectural preservation of which buildings have to be protected and to which point in their past existence they have to return. Rather than being an expression of naive nostalgia, these decisions are informed by governing canons that entail the politicized and polarizing rummage of prime specimens of architecture, usually located in strategic locations of high economic value. As such, when the state of decay — of imminent death and mourning — has been officialized by the system, conservation becomes a priority. As a personal project, the taxidermy of animals and representation of nature in the African Hall are related to Theodore Roosevelt's territorial policies that established national parks, forests, monuments, and even his own memorial in front of the Museum. The early diagnosis of neurasthenia, a type of boredom resulting from urbanization and industrialization, encouraged the president — the "Teddy Bear" that titles Haraway's investigation[11] — to explore the outdoors and be physically active, in exclusive communion with other men.[12]

Epitomized by the aim to protect nature — "the restoration of the origin, the task of genetic hygiene"[13] — preservation suggests that the urban present is so polluted and deteriorated that it requires the past to progress. Although the mission is to extend the previous, paradoxically the previous is erased. A building that has gone through a process of preservation, either by being renovated or by being altered through cuts or additions, has a new beginning that marks a new temporality. To arrest decadence and produce permanence, these interventions re-synchronize the object, forcing it to reach the level of development and rationalization imposed by the political and economic apparatus that allowed its transformation. Similar to Akeley's conviction that by immortalizing the best samples of African fauna further destruction could be avoided,[14] the survival offered by preservation appears heroic, rescuing buildings from early demises, with educational purposes and optimizing resources. Nonetheless, the modes of production of preservation defer to the hegemonic forces that allow its materialization, as unveiled by Haraway in the racism and gender inequality that shaped the dioramas of the African Hall. In the same way, the improvement of technologies of mapping, cleaning, and environmental control provides accuracy in the recovery of the past and facilitates scientific and historical research. However, they are also part of a system concerned with capital gain, industrial development, and political power — like Akeley's improvements of photographic and filmic techniques that, due to their superiority "to the gun for the control of time,"[15] were adopted equally by Hollywood studios and the US Department of War.[16]

### Considering Boredom
Due to the need of recovering investment and obtaining profit, the developers of preservation favor the monumental and what is considered

the outcome of architectural genius, disregarding the repetitious and mundane — the boring — and overlooking that what is left to perish is as significant in the understanding of history as what is allowed to survive. To enlighten the criteria of preservation, Fredric Jameson commends boredom as "a very useful instrument with which to explore the past, and to stage a meeting between it and the present."[17] By exhausting the celebrated — becoming bored with the "classics" — attention can be given to what has been forgotten, the non-survivors that did not qualify for posterity because they, at the moment of their estimation, were perceived as irrelevant.

Like the omission of Akeley's wives and the Africans of his convoys in the official version of the Museum, boredom problematizes the role of the past in the construction of the future. Its fixation with the present resonates with preservation in a twofold way. On the one hand, the aspiration of the African Hall to exhibit nature as the most pristine past, the interest with historicity, consumed images, and former styles fuels a pervasive sense of ahistoricity.[18] The craving for the actualization of the previous through acts of preservation responds to the need of filling the emptiness of the present, incapable of producing meaning and questioning the progressivist conviction that a better future can be assembled. Former configurations supply an endless source of positive material, already scrutinized and approved, with marginal risk of failure or inefficiency. On the other hand, according to Emil Cioran, the interest with history, its recording and salvation is the result of the fear of boredom — of repeating endlessly what has been done and achieved. By implication, boredom ought to be the starting point from which the past should be investigated, turning history into a text that indicates what should be evaded.[19]

If architectural preservation is compared to moments of boredom — when the present stops providing difference, in between "that which happens" and "that which fails to occur"[20] — then the dragging of yesterday into today can be incorporated in the innovation of the future. Rather than providing a passive account of the past, preservation can structure a critical threshold — in between temporalities and spaces —

where what has not been imagined yet can emerge, promoting forming and disregarding fixed representations of the future.[21] Unlike the prescriptive dioramas of the African Hall, the dismantling of the façade of the American Folk Art Museum, or the skinning of the Farwell Building, preservation can turn into an act of inclusion, surpassing the nostalgia shared with taxidermy and merging with architecture as a whole.

## Notes

1 John Freeman Gill, "The Folly of Saving What You Kill," *The New York Times* (2014).

2 Blair Kamin, "The Danger of Becoming Skin Deep," *Chicago Tribune* (2007). Academic elaborations have also used the metaphor of taxidermy to critique certain approaches to preservation. See for example, Steven W. Semes, *The Future of the Past: A Conservation Ethic for Architecture, Urbanism, and Historic Preservation* (New York: W. W. Norton, 2009), 239; Anika S. Lemar, "Zoning as Taxidermy: Neighborhood Conservation Districts and the Regulation of Aesthetics," *Indiana Law Journal* 90, no. 4 (2015).

3 "Taxidermy," in *The Shorter Oxford English Dictionary*, ed. C. T. Onions (Oxford: Clarendon Press, 1972), vol. II, 2250.

4 "Akeley Hall of African Mammals," American Museum of National History, http://www.amnh.org/exhibitions/permanent-exhibitions/mammal-halls/akeley-hall-of-african-mammals.

5 Ibid.

6 Donna Haraway, "Teddy Bear Patriarchy: Taxidermy in the Garden of Eden, New York City, 1908–1936," *Social Text* 11 (1984): 21.

7 Ibid., 48.

8 Ibid., 20.

9 Ibid., 21.

10 Ibid., 54.

11 Haraway explains in a footnote, "The Deavereaux or Hotel Colorado in Glenwood Springs, CO, contains a plaque with one version of the origin of the Teddy Bear, emblem of Theodor Roosevelt: T.R. returned empty handed from a hunting trip to the hotel, and so a hotel maid created a little stuffed bear and gave it to him. ... Another version has T.R. sparing the life of a bear cub, with the stuffed version commemorating his kindness." Ibid., 58.

12    Anne Stiles, "Go Rest, Young Man," *Monitor on Psychology* 43, no. 1 (2012), http://www.apa.org/monitor/2012/01/go-rest.aspx. In female sufferers, the same condition was treated through domiciliary confinement. Allison Pease, *Modernism, Feminism, and the Culture of Boredom* (Cambridge: Cambridge University Press, 2012), 25.

13    Haraway, "Teddy Bear Patriarchy," 20.

14    Haraway remarks that Akeley was aware of the destruction caused by his presence in Africa: "After his first visit in 1921, he was motivated to convince the Belgian government to make of this area the first African national park to ensure an absolute sanctuary for the gorilla in the future." Ibid., 25.

15    Ibid., 42.

16    Mark Alvey, "The Cinema as Taxidermy: Carl Akeley and the Preservative Obsession," *Framework* 48, no. 1 (2007).

17    Fredric Jameson, *Postmodernism, or, the Cultural Logic of Late Capitalism* (London: Verso, 1991), 303.

18    Ibid., 71–72.

19    Emil Cioran, *History and Utopia*, trans. Richard Howard (New York: Seaver, 1987), 109; *Tears and Saints*, trans. Ilinca Zarifopol-Johnston (Chicago: University of Chicago Press, 1995), 86.

20    Patrice Petro, *Aftershocks of the New: Feminism and Film History* (New Brunswick: Rutgers University Press, 2002), 57.

21    Andrew Benjamin, "Boredom and Distraction: The Moods of Modernity," in *Walter Benjamin and History*, ed. Andrew Benjamin (London: Continuum, 2005), 170.

Christian Parreno is a PhD Fellow at the Oslo School of Architecture and Design.

**Superstructure**
Yona Friedman,
Ville Spatiale, 1958–2006

**Mat**
Candilis Josic Woods,
Reconstruction of the Center
of Frankfurt-Römerberg, 1963

**Monolith**
Superstudio,
The Continuous Monument, 1969

**Composite**
Lina Bo Bardi,
SESC Pompéia, 1982

**Envelope**
Bernard Tschumi,
Fresnoy Art Center, 1991–97

**Shape**
Xaveer de Geyter Architects,
Square Rogier, 2006–15

**Stitching**
Mansilla + Tuñón,
Atrio Hotel, 2005–10

**Frame**
José María Sánchez García,
Templo de Diana, 2011

**Skin**
OMA,
Fondazione Prada, 2015

**Partition**
Dogma,
Pretty Vacant, 2014

**Threshold**
MVRDV,
The Unifying Ring and
the Norwegian Garden, 2015

# Form

# Superstructure

## Yona Friedman
### Ville Spatiale, 1958–2006

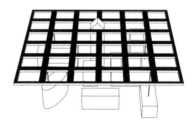

Hovering over existing cities, Yona Friedman's Ville Spatiale proposes a flexible infrastructural system for new construction. In contrast to the large-scale demolition of urban renewal, this system locates housing and social spaces above extant urban conditions, producing a vertically stacked coexistence of new and old architecture. In addition to its social agenda of flexible self-built housing, the project shows how new architecture can float as an elevated roof above urban landscapes, albeit with significant challenges for daylight and structural support. Connecting across multiple buildings, the superstructure changes the part-to-whole relationship of existing buildings and their cities. Undoing the autonomy of such monuments as the Centre Pompidou and Les Halles, the system pulls individual historic buildings into an integrated city-scale structure.

Yona Friedman, Umbrella for Les Halles, Paris, 1969

Friedman depicts the superstructure transforming
the nineteenthth-century glass-and-iron structure of
Les Halles in Paris. Revealing a resonance with Victor
Baltard's language of iron structural frames, the image
suggests how the new elevated construction can extend
the structural and formal language of existing buildings.

Yona Friedman, Paris Spatiale, Paris, 1959

In this image of a Parisian street, the
superstructure forms a new ceiling for the existing
urban condition, turning building façades into walls
of a larger urban room.

This depiction of the Ville Spatiale over the
Seine shows it as a second urban ground, equal in
expansiveness and scale to the landscape below.
Compositionally, the image even accentuates the
similarity by mirroring the superstructure and the
Seine over the horizon line.

# Mat

**———**

## Candilis Josic Woods
### Reconstruction of the Center of Frankfurt-Römerberg, 1963

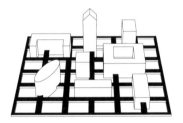

In one of their characteristic mat building projects, Georges Candilis, Alexis Josic, and Shadrach Woods propose an adaptable horizontal structure to fill the voids between existing buildings in Frankfurt. Responding to the historic city center, which was heavily bombed in WWII, this reconstruction abstracts the scale of the city blocks into an orthogonal grid of indoor and outdoor spaces. The new structure wraps around and between the remaining historic buildings, deflecting the outer edges of its grid to attach to their surfaces. While the structure ostensibly references the local city blocks, its primary impression is as a new ground for the remaining historic buildings. Like Yona Friedman's Ville Spatiale, this project turns individual buildings into parts of an urban-scale megastructure, but this time enacting transformation on the ground plane.

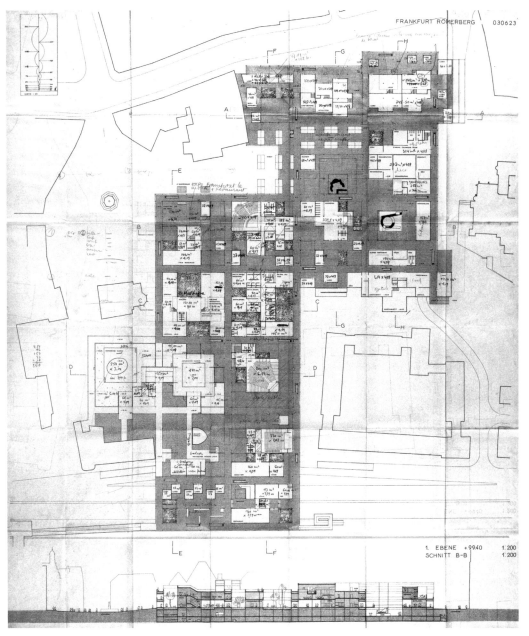

FRANKFURT RÖMERBERG          030623

1. EBENE +9940          1:200
SCHNITT B-B          1:200

Candilis Josic Woods, Plan for the reconstruction of the center of Frankfurt-Römerberg, 1963

The plan highlights the integration of social functions, outdoor space, and circulation paths within the structure, as well as its deflection to match the forms of surrounding buildings.

Form

Candilis Josic Woods, Reconstruction of the center of Frankfurt-Römerberg, 1963

The new grid structure abstracts and multiplies
the traditional city block form of perimeter buildings
surrounding an inner courtyard. The layered
multiplication of this perimeter type produces complex
patterns of solid and void spaces, as in the firm's
contemporaneous proposal for the Free University
of Berlin.

This view of the competition model foregrounds the system's ability to wrap around existing structures, such as the moment where a monument protrudes from an inner courtyard. As with other mat building projects, it is easy to imagine the structure expanding outwards to interlock further with its surrounding context.

# Monolith

**———**

## Superstudio
The Continuous Monument, 1969

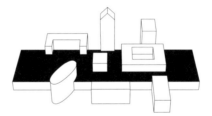

Superstudio's Continuous Monument project — an imagined, gridded monolith that stretched across the globe — is often explained as a parody of late modernism. While some of the images emphasize the contrast between the monolith and its surroundings, others, such as the two that follow, show it interlocking with existing architecture. As with Superstudio's later "Salvages of Italian Historic Centers" — a direct engagement with Italian preservation politics — these images complicate the parody of modernism with a jab at contextualism. The images show a playful alternative to the contextualism of mimetic material and scale, by depicting a massive abstract form that adjusts its envelope and perimeters to the contours of the existing. The result can be read either as a parody of modernist concessions to context, or as a provocation to explore the intersection of large-scale abstraction with local specificity.

Superstudio, "Manhattan," from The Continuous Monument, photomontage, 1969

In both images, the geometry of the monolith
adjusts to the specificities of Manhattan's towers. In
the first image, the monolith appears as a thin shell,
with its bottom edge precisely fitting existing buildings
and with the low buildings penetrating its interior.
In the second image, the gridded box loses its pure
geometry and distorts into extrusions of the skyline.

Superstudio, "New York extrusion," from The Continuous
Monument, photomontage, 1969

# Composite

## Lina Bo Bardi
### SESC Pompéia, 1982

In her transformation of a former factory complex in São Paulo, Brazil, Lina Bo Bardi inserted new concrete forms to create spaces of social interaction. Throughout the project, she transforms factory buildings with new insertions that have equal spatial and visual importance to the existing. At the scale of the site, towers adjacent to the original buildings compete visually with the red brick factory structures through their striking concrete façades and red apertures. On the interiors, massive concrete forms produce enclosures for seating and programming, their own scale responding to the expansive scale of the factory halls. Rather than implementing a totalizing formal coherence, this project produces an exterior and interior composite, in which new forms are spatially interspersed and interwoven with existing structures. Typical of Bo Bardi's work, this project used architectural reuse as an instrument for social regeneration, producing a highly successful space for both cultural and athletic activity.

Lina Bo Bardi, SESC Pompéia, São Paulo, 1982

Lina Bo Bardi, SESC Pompéia, São Paulo, 1982

Bo Bardi's composite strategy operates at all
scales, from new exterior volumes to the interior
furniture and this transformation of the ground plane
through a meandering body of water. Her use of strong
geometric shapes creates coherence between the new
insertions and visual connections across disparate
parts of the factory buildings.

Bo Bardi's use of bright colored paint and rough concrete creates a field of different textures, in which the brick of the factory buildings and the new board-formed concrete walls rival each other in richness and complexity.

# Envelope

## Bernard Tschumi
## Fresnoy Art Center, 1991–97

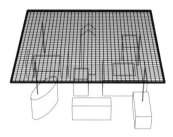

In transforming a leisure complex from the 1920s into a contemporary arts space, Bernard Tschumi Architects used a new envelope to coalesce disparate buildings into a single institution. The original leisure buildings were kept for their large-scale spaces, but a massive, high-peformance roof supplements them with new mechanical systems. Spatially, the roof creates a coherent container for the different structures, as well as a new interstitial space for circulation and social events. Former roofs become floors, and a network of stairs and pathways produces playful event spaces in this zone of spatial inversion.

Bernard Tschumi Architects, Le Fresnoy National Studio for Contemporary Arts, Tourcoing, France, 1991–97

The two open façades reveal the disparate
buildings subsumed under a new roof structure, along
with the disconnect between the old rooflines and the
geometry of the new shell.

Bernard Tschumi Architects, Le Fresnoy National Studio for Contemporary Arts, Tourcoing, France, 1991–97

The contrast between the industrial roof and the
discrete existing buildings sets up a tension between
part and whole, diversity and coherence, similar to the
effect of Yona Friedman's Ville Spatiale over Paris.

Elevated to the level of the rooftops, the network of circulation paths produces a social zone in a setting of spatial inversion. Paths cross former rooftops that appear as grounds, and individual buildings recede into a field of oblique surfaces.

# Shape

## Xaveer de Geyter Architects
### Square Rogier, 2006–15

Addressing a complex knot of metro and bus lines, public space, and existing buildings, Xaveer de Geyter creates a new connecting hub articulated by a circular form. The Square Rogier addresses infrastructure on several underground levels, tying together layers of horizontal movement. Multiple, crossing pathways converge on a point of vertical circulation, which brings pedestrians up to a public plaza capped by a circular canopy. Here, the Platonic form of the circle articulates the moment of convergence, and creates a visual and spatial focal point in a site of diverse existing buildings, street traffic, and vertical circulation.

Xaveer de Geyter Architects, Square Rogier, Brussels, 2006–15

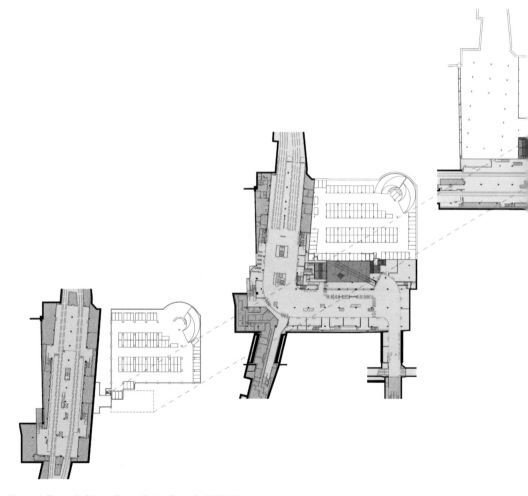

Xaveer de Geyter Architects, Square Rogier, Brussels, 2006–15

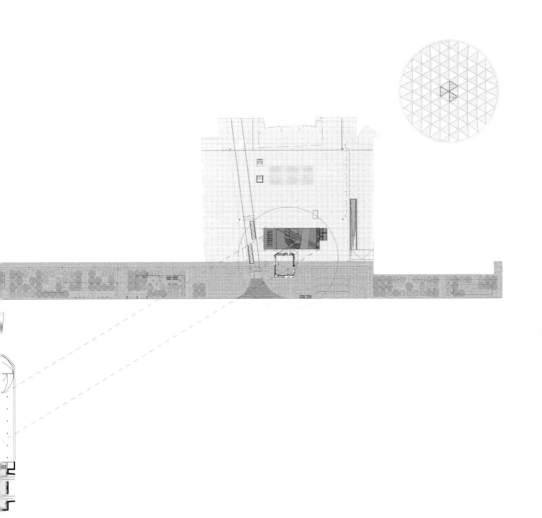

The exploded plan drawings of the project
demonstrate the multiple directions of movement that
cross below ground, and how the circular form caps
their moment of intersection.

# Stitching

---

## Mansilla + Tuñón
## Atrio Hotel, 2005–10

While many of these case studies use overarching geometry to produce coherence at the scale of the site, this project by Mansilla + Tuñón deploys individual structural elements to give legibility to interstitial social space. Connecting several existing stone buildings in the medieval section of Cáceres, Spain, the architects articulated the courtyard space between them with a language of repeating white concrete columns. Serving as both structure and façade, these white vertical lines tie together disparate buildings with a consistent visual language, even as they weave in and out of irregular spaces. Demarcating both exterior and interior social spaces, this language transforms in the ground-floor restaurant into vertical wood elements with the same increment of repetition.

Mansilla + Tuñón, Relais & Châteaux Atrio, Cáceres, courtyard view, 2005–10

Mansilla + Tuñón, Relais & Châteaux Atrio, Cáceres, atrium view, 2005–10

Addressing the challenges of drawing interstitial projects, Mansilla + Tuñón developed strategies for depicting the interlocking of existing and new construction through an exploded axonometric.

# Frame
José María Sánchez García
## Templo de Diana, 2011

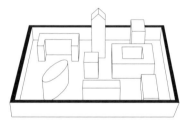

In designing a visitors' center and viewing platform for the
Roman Temple of Diana in Mérida, Spain, José María Sánchez
García produced a series of spatial framing devices. Layers
of public space frame the temple structure — a perimeter of open
ground, a viewing platform, and enclosed program rooms. Each
of these layers offers a different form of movement and interaction
with the temple, from physical to optical to mediated perception
through apertures. Emphasizing inward focus towards the temple,
the formal language of the architecture changes dramatically
from center to periphery. The inner orthogonal frames contrast
sharply with the peripheral edges, which match the irregularity
of the surrounding context. The outer ring of rooms and light wells
deflects to fit into the interstitial spaces of surrounding buildings.
Through layers of planometric and sectional frames, this austere
structure stages a sequence of visual and tactile interactions
with an ancient monument.

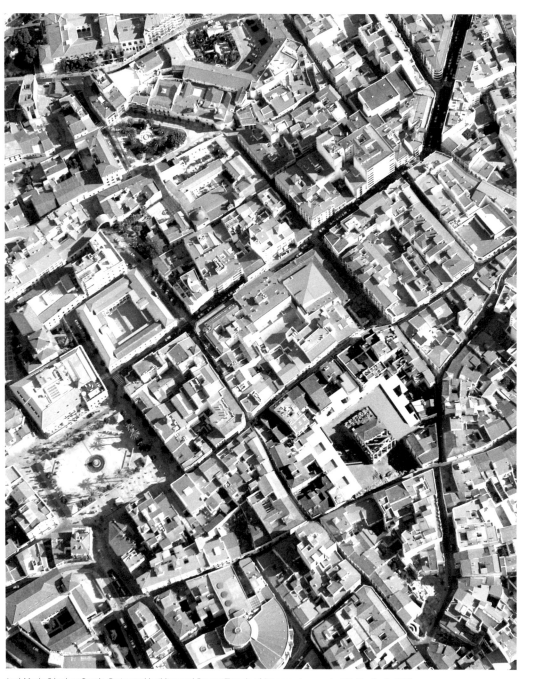

José María Sánchez García, Perimetral building and Roman Temple of Diana environments, Mérida, Spain, 2011

In the aerial view, the contrast is most apparent between the inner orthogonal frame around the temple and the rear side, which interlocks with the complexity of its surroundings.

José María Sánchez García, Perimetral building and Roman Temple of Diana environments, Mérida, Spain, 2011

The building's alternating pattern of solids and voids, program volumes and light wells, both mimics the forms of the surrounding buildings and offers a system capable of interlocking with them.

The viewing platform cantilevers to the same level
as the temple floor, producing both visual continuity
and discontinuity in the space between old and new
structures.

José María Sánchez García, Perimetral building and Roman Temple of Diana environments, Mérida, Spain, 2011

The project frames not only the temple but
also the surrounding archaeological remains, which
are bracketed by the vertical rhythm of columns
and light wells.

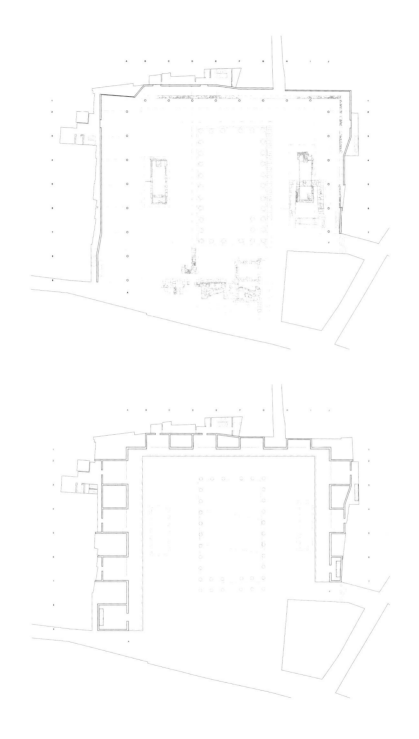

## Skin

---

# OMA

## Fondazione Prada, 2015

The recent Fondazione Prada complex in Milan by OMA inverts the trope of façadism in reuse and preservation. The façades of historic buildings are often kept intact and their interiors gutted, maintaining the outside image of stasis and hiding change. This project instead transforms historic façades and interiors through surface alchemy, broadcasting the process of transformation. The complex includes both repurposed and new buildings, each of which display a façade of heightened textural richness. The Haunted House building, entirely covered in gold leaf, is the most obvious example, but even the exterior mirror on the Cinema building and the spotless stucco façades that resemble stage sets undermine any easy distinctions between old and new. The new surfaces create a complex of sensorial intensity and unstable temporal identity.

OMA, Fondazione Prada, Milan, 2015

The Haunted House building most clearly demonstrates surface alchemy, maintaining changes in surface depth, but introducing new properties of luminosity and texture.

OMA, Fondazione Prada, Milan, 2015

From across the street, the many heightened
textures of the project appear, including not only the
gold leaf skin and stuccoed factory buildings, but also
the aluminum foam façade of the new Podium building.

The mirror on the façade of the Cinema building
plays further with materiality and dematerialization,
dissolving the façade of its building into a reflection
of the surrounding former factory buildings.

# Partition

---

## Dogma
## Pretty Vacant, 2014

Known for investigating forms of absolute architecture, Dogma has more recently developed proposals for transforming specific existing structures. Looking at the quantity of vacant office buildings in the Quartier Léopold in Brussels, Dogma proposes converting open office plans into new models of live-work spaces. Questioning the convention of the single-family home and its normative implications for domestic life, the Pretty Vacant project inserts living units within larger fields of flexible work space, encouraging both communal living and working. In this specific case study on Rue Belliard, the transformation operates at the scale of both architecture and urbanism, with living units that create partitions for domestic space within each floor plate and towers that reorganize a perimeter block into larger units of communal space.

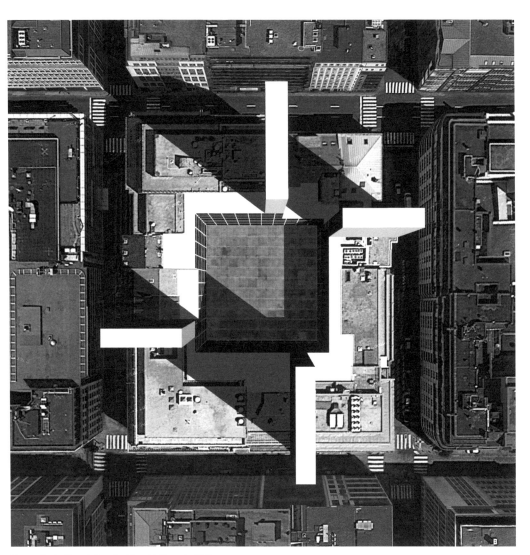

Dogma, Pretty Vacant, Quartier Léopold, Brussels, 2014

Transforming an entire block of office buildings, four new towers subdivide the complex into large segments and bring circulation into the central courtyard, where balconies connect along the inner edge of the courtyard to form shared social spaces.

Dogma, Pretty Vacant, Quartier Léopold, Brussels, 2014

The reorganization of the block, both through
the towers and the interior partitions, creates a tension
between simultaneous architectural continuity and
social transformation at the urban scale.

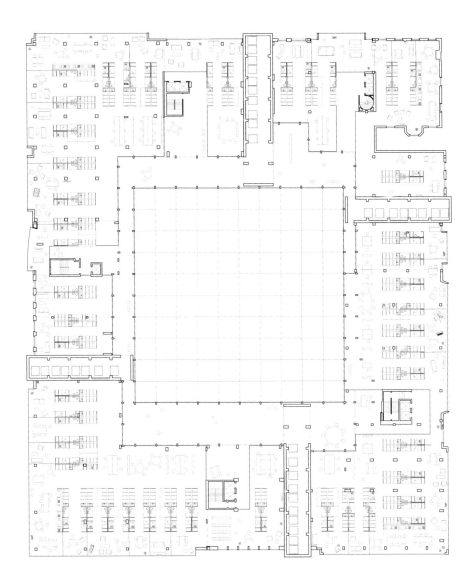

Within each floor plate, smaller "wall elements" create a rhythm of partitions with essential living functions — kitchens, bathrooms, dining tables, and beds. The interspersal of living units within communal work space is intended to provide the support of shared domestic labor.

# Threshold

---

## MVRDV
## The Unifying Ring and
## the Norwegian Garden, 2015

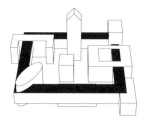

For the ideas phase of planning the new Norwegian national government quarter in Oslo, discussed in the following Case Study section, the MVRDV team confronted conventions for both preservation and spaces of government. The team began with a series of provocative diagrams, challenging the isolation and legibility of individual monuments — an earth mound, a wall, an eclectic pile, a repetition of the conventional European block, etc. The final proposal pursued two tandem strategies — a wall of programming that wraps around the site, and an inner garden with ghost traces of buildings that had been demolished. The wall exaggerates the conventional isolation of the landmark structure in its center, while physically merging with buildings at the perimeter. This project gambles with the political trope of the fortress, exaggerating the client's desire for secure fortification while making its top surface and center into publicly accessible park spaces.

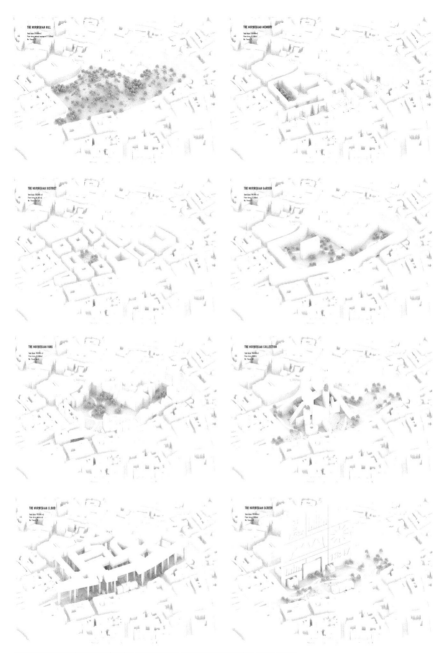

MVRDV, Initial diagrams for the government quarter master plan, Oslo, 2015

The initial diagrams offer eight contrasting strategies for redesigning the government district, all questioning the object of preservation. Each proposal maintains a different aspect of the site while disregarding others, focusing in turn on the landscape, the footprints of existing buildings, the surrounding urban form, or data about the city.

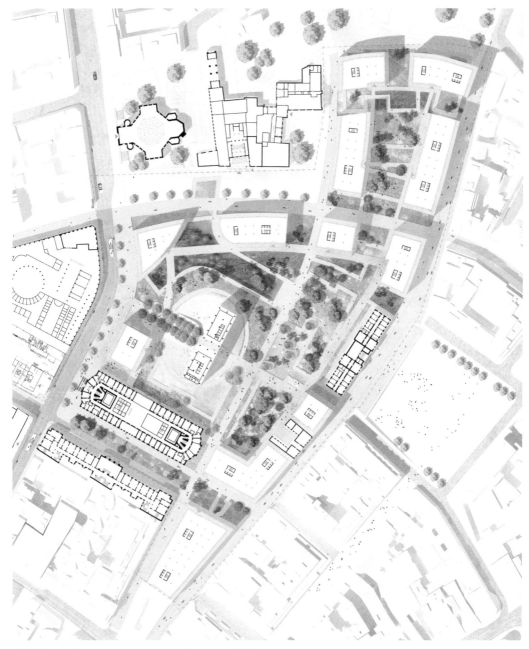

MVRDV, The Unifying Ring and the Norwegian Garden, Oslo, 2015

In the inner garden, pathways show the layered history of the site, marking the outlines of buildings that the government approved for demolition. Toying with tropes of memorialization, the pathways make a palimpsest into a network of physical movement.

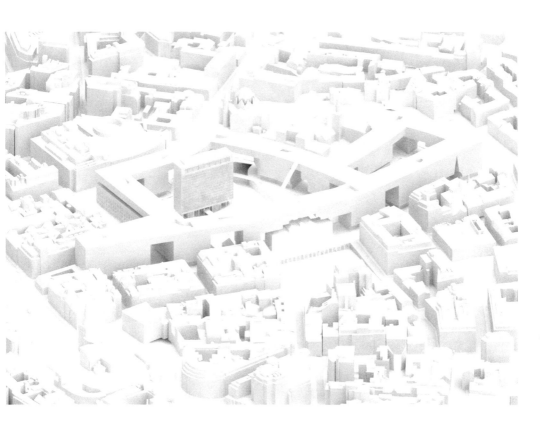

The Unifying Ring, or wall around the site,
challenges conventions about the isolation and
legibility of historical monuments. Politically, it asserts
a bold separation of the government quarter from the
rest of the city, producing an inner garden distinct from
its surroundings. As a preservation device, the wall
both upholds a conventional isolation of the central
object, the Høyblokka building, and subverts the
legibility of the surrounding buildings. Hovering over
and wrapping around the perimeter buildings, both
extant and demolished, the wall exaggerates the iconic
profiles of these buildings, fundamentally disrupting
their legibility as individual monuments.

**Introduction to the Government Quarter**
Bryony Roberts

**Utopia and Conservation**
Erik Langdalen

**Mediation and Preservation**
Mattias Ekman

**Site Images**

**Open Quarter Master Plan**
AHO and GSAPP Team

# Case Study

# Introduction to the Government Quarter

## Bryony Roberts

The controversial planning process for the national government district in Oslo, Norway, in the spring of 2015 foregrounded the political agency of preservation. The government district, which houses the ministry offices of the executive branch and the office of the Prime Minister, was profoundly transformed after the terrorist attack by Anders Breivik on July 22, 2011. Intended as a distraction before his rampage on Utøya island, Breivik's car bomb in front of the Høyblokka killed eight people and blew out the façades of surrounding buildings. The Høyblokka and adjacent Y-blokka buildings remained structurally intact, a testament to their design by mid-century modernist Erling Viksjø, but heated debates about memorialization, preservation, and growth kept the site half-vacant and in limbo for years. Following several government assessment studies, the Norwegian Directorate of Public Construction and Property (Statsbygg)

AHO student Ida Nordstrøm
presenting the AHO Team project
to Minister Jan Tore Sanner,
April 13, 2015

initiated a highly visible ideas phase for the planning of the government quarter, inviting six lead offices to submit ideas — Snøhetta, MVRDV, Bjarke Ingels Group (BIG), LPO, White, and Asplan Viak. Invited by Statsbygg to participate in the planning process, the Oslo School of Architecture (AHO) established a collaboration with the Columbia Graduate School of Planning and Preservation (GSAPP). This collaborative group, which I led in consultation with Erik Langdalen and Jorge Otero-Pailos, submitted a proposal with a focus on preservation and reuse. The ideas phase and the ensuing public debates threw into relief the limitations of the planning process and the need to address the historical dimensions of the site in forming a new representation of the Norwegian government.

The premises of the Statsbygg ideas phase (*parallelloppdrag*) were themselves controversial, as they required the demolition of several central buildings and the massive addition of new office space. The *parallelloppdrag* followed decisions to concentrate most ministry offices in the government district, to plan for large future growth, and to favor new construction rather than reuse. The brief required 115,000 square meters of office space by 2034, and an additional 62,500 square meters by 2064, the equivalent of approximately two million square feet in the space of two large city blocks. To accommodate this new density, Statsbygg decided to demolish the Y-blokka building, part of the Høyblokka, and several of the surrounding office buildings to make space for new towers. This top-down plan within a culture of democratic and consensual decision-making ignited ongoing protests from architects, architectural historians, and citizens concerned about sudden densification. In the *parallelloppdrag*, the professional teams were required to comply with these conditions in order to avoid being disqualified, even if they personally supported the preservation of Viksjø's buildings and harbored concerns about dramatic changes in density. Though also requred to comply, our academic team took advantage of our financial independence, deciding to follow our convictions and use our project to publicly challenge the planning premises.

The ideas phase took place as a series of collective seminars, in which the six professional teams and our academic team gave

Monumental field of the government quarter, with buildings for ministry offices, press, unions, courts, police, and other functions

presentations and discussed strategies with the evaluating committee and representatives from local and national government. This process seemed, at least in its structure, to encourage meta discussions about the role of architecture in addressing symbolism, trauma, and national identity. Unfortunately, the discussions were primarily focused on issues of security, transportation infrastructure, and maximizing office area. The historical value of the existing architecture and the potential for reuse were given only fleeting attention, and any attempts to question the decisions about demolition were quickly dismissed. In this climate, it became clear that any effort to posit strategies for activating the Høyblokka, preserving the Y-blokka, and integrating the modernist buildings into their network of surrounding historical structures would need to become a project of resistance.

The resulting project served as a protest against the assumptions of the planning process and posited a relational interdependence of new and existing architecture. As our team discovered on further analysis, the government district is a monumental field that offers an unusual and valuable representation of governance. The government district consists of buildings of diverse time periods and styles, sampling a succession of architectural ambitions for representing governmental authority. The rusticated Gamleblokka building by Henrik Bull from 1906 sits alongside the postwar modernist forms of the Høyblokka and Y-blokka. Interspersed within the complex of ministry buildings are also buildings for other cultural and governmental institutions, such as the Deichmanske Library, Trinity Church, newspaper offices, and union headquarters. The result is a space of government that represented the diversity of both architectural history and political institutions in Norwegian society. One of the main ambitions of the AHO Team project was to maintain the diversity of this monumental field even as it expanded to include new office space.

In order to accommodate the massive new area of office space and improve urban circulation while maintaining architectural diversity, our team focused on altering the ground plane. Inspired by some of the radical projects represented earlier in this book, the team looked for

Public debates over the team proposals in *Aftenposten*, April 14, 2015

large-scale interventions that could give coherence to the space of government while also allowing for a multiplicity of time periods. Looking closely at the ground plane, we realized that we could both activate and preserve the existing buildings by inserting a new datum beneath them. As a result, we designed a thickened ground plane for some of the new office space, but punctured that ground with large garden atriums that would bring in light and air. Our team challenged the sudden densification of the site through proposing different construction phasing, which would build out the entire site for the first phase by 2034, distributing the office area in lower-scale structures, as well as maximizing the reuse of existing structures. The new buildings would then be renovated in 2064 using smartworking and flexible office solutions, learning from the next fifty years of technological innovation. The result was a lower-scale complex of buildings at approximately the same height as the central Høyblokka. The design of the ground plane and the arrangement of the new buildings both responded to the existing compositional logic of the site and built on the qualities of an urban conservation utopia that Erik Langdalen discusses in the following essay.

We presented this project in a climate of heated public debates and protests against the demolition of the Y-blokka. Knowing that none of the other teams were offering solutions for integrating the Y-blokka into the new construction, we felt it was our responsibility as architects and preservationists to show this possibility. We presented our solution to Statsbygg in the final seminar of the *parallelloppdrag*, and despite their displeasure, they allowed us to exhibit it in the Høyblokka pavilion alongside the other proposals. Although the images of our project were initially not released to the press, newspapers and television news programs nonetheless tracked down images and began promoting the project. The project quickly gained large public support and frequently placed second in national polls about the proposals, because of its integrated scale and preservation of the Y-blokka. The planning process progressed as originally intended, with the ideas from the teams streamlined into a singular plan put forward by Statsbygg. However, in June 2015, Statsbygg released statements that they would lower

Public protest to save the Y-blokka building, Oslo,
February 9, 2015

the density of the new development so that the Høyblokka would be the
tallest building. It remains unclear if our project had a direct effect on
that decision, but we hope that in articulating public interests through
images of alternative density, we prompted a reconsideration of the
government's assumptions. Unfortunately, the Y-blokka building still
remains slated for demolition.

In the essay that follows, Erik Langdalen, the Head of the Institute of
Form, Theory and History at AHO, discusses the history of the government
district and how it exemplifies the conception of an urban conservation
utopia. As we were developing the project, we discovered that Erling
Viksjø's architecture was operating in response to the surrounding
historical buildings, and Langdalen expands on this observation to advocate
for continued responsive design on the site. Mattias Ekman contributes
an essay based on his PhD at AHO on the role of mediation in changing
preservation decisions about the government district. Together they reveal
the entangled political associations of the site and the significance of
preserving its architecture. Following these texts, historical images of the
government district and images from our design proposal expand on the
possibilities for activating the site's historical structures.

# Utopia and Conservation

## Erik Langdalen

The terrorist bombing of the government quarter in Oslo on July 22, 2011, did not only cause the tragic death of eight people and severe material damage; it also left the central part of downtown Oslo in a state of uncertainty. The recently agreed-upon plan to list the two central, postwar government buildings designed by architect Erling Viksjø, Høyblokka (1959) and Y-blokka (1970), was unexpectedly brought into question. So was the long-established idea of a dispersed governmental quarter and a medium-scaled, diversified urban landscape. The 2015 call for ideas that resulted in seven proposals for a new consolidated government quarter (for 2025 and 2064 respectively) implied extraordinary density, high security, and the demolition of Y-blokka, premises that would completely redefine the urban landscape of Oslo. When confronted by the proposals of the six preselected international teams, one is struck by the confidence the teams demonstrate when predicting a fifty-year-long urban development and the desire to project one coherent architectural vision into the future. Considering the complex history of the Hammersborg area, where the government quarter is situated, it is peculiar that none of the teams (or the client) seemed to take into account the many compromises, changes of requirements, and unexpected events that already have taken place and most likely will occur in the future. Yet most striking is the absence of ideas for a reimagined historic city. There seems to be an assumed contradiction between architectural imagination and urban conservation: conservation is considered to deal exclusively with the past, is rarely seen as a creative practice, and is reduced to an aspect of architecture and urban planning. There is an urgent need to trace the history of urban conservation in order to reformulate the discipline of urban planning.

In *The Historic Urban Landscape: Managing Heritage in an Urban Century*, Francesco Bandarin and Ron van Oers make the compelling argument that urban conservation is a modern utopia, on equal terms with the canonical twentieth-century utopias authored by Tony Garnier, Ebenezer Howard, Le Corbusier, Frank Lloyd Wright, and others. Their claim is that urban conservation is "steeped in legend," aiming to safeguard the integrity and the authenticity of the historic city, though always remaining "an aspiration that is subject to continuous compromise and adaption." Bandarin and van Oers argue that "if utopias are thought of as collective representations of communities or societies, idealized conditions expressing shared value systems and common goals, then defining urban conservation as a utopia becomes a positive and constructive approach."[1] When taking this as a point of departure, what are the implications of naming urban conservation a utopia?

What characterizes a utopia are its radical and projective properties, conceived through the creative act of an author. Conservation is perceived as the opposite: conservative, retrospective, and rarely defined as an act of creativity. The idea of conservation as a utopic practice suggests instead that urban conservation is as much about the future as the past, is as radical as any other utopia, and is undisputedly a creative act.

Utopias have the thrilling effect of electrifying the present, shaking our known world and evoking images of a distant future. The effect is obtained by establishing a discrepancy between *now* and *then*. The larger the discrepancy, the greater the effect, and the more utopian the utopia turns out to be. While the utopias of modernism relied on the shock of demolition and replacement, the utopia of urban conservation relies on recharging the existing: a contamination of familiar objects, buildings, and cities, charging what is familiar with new meaning and projecting them into the future.

An architectural utopia is governed by *practices* conceived according to certain principles, modes of operation, and representational techniques. These practices aim to correspond to the radical nature of the utopia, normally by abandoning the conventions of the realities that the utopia is both opposed to and rooted in. Urban conservation practices operate differently: they aim to infiltrate rather than to abandon, to unravel mysteries rather than to invent new ones, and consequently to create synthesis rather than separation.

So who are the authors of urban conservation utopias, and what are the practices they deploy?

Among the earliest and most prominent examples of urban conservation is the work of the influential Italian architectural historian, restorer, architect, civil engineer, and urban planner Gustavo Giovannoni (1873-1947). He formulated what is considered the first comprehensive concept of urban conservation, parallel to, and possibly an alternative to the known utopias of modernism. According to the French architectural and urban historian Françoise Choay, "[Giovannoni] grants to the ancient urban ensembles both a use value and a museal value by integrating them into a general conception of territorial planning and development."[2] He reinforced the historic district as a legitimate entity of cultural heritage, but unlike his forerunners, he took into account the challenges of the industrialized city: accelerating traffic, unsanitary slums, and severe pollution. In contrast to the idea of urban sanitation, as manifested by Baron Haussmann's transformation of Paris, he proposed a kind of "urban acupuncture," allowing the systems of modernity to flow through the historic city. He introduced a set of architectural strategies on a small-scale level that

enabled a mediation between the historic city and the demands of modern life. According to the architectural historian Lucia Allais, Giovannoni "sought to make monument restoration a true expression of our age, through the application of modern materials. ... Giovannoni saw restoration as a path to an alternate modernity, more modern than modernism itself."[3] Gustavo Giovannoni was instrumental in turning urban conservation into an international movement organized according to universal agreements, charters, and legislation. He was a key player at the 1931 *First International Congress of Architects and Technicians of Historic Monuments*, which resulted in the highly influential *Athens Charter for the Restoration of Historic Monuments*.

Also present at the congress in Athens was the Norwegian delegate Harry Fett (1875-1962), who was the Director General of the Norwegian Directorate of Cultural Heritage from 1913 to 1945 and unquestionably the most influential figure in the formation of a comprehensive Norwegian conservation policy. Fett met Givannoni in Athens, and he certainly absorbed the ideas that circulated at the Congress. When Fett returned to Norway, he established a conservation policy very much in line with Giovannoni's ideas, resulting in the protection of significant urban environments like the historic city of Røros, the Kirkeristen in Oslo, and the piers of Bergen. Fett advocated protection of historic environments rather than single buildings and monuments.[4] He considered historic buildings an integral part of the contemporary city, belonging as much to the present as to the past,[5] and proposed specific architectural strategies that integrated historical structures with new ones. Harry Fett's contribution to the intense debate that accompanied the planning process of a new government building in Oslo in the 1940s and '50s is well known, but the impact his urban conservation ideas had on the result has not been sufficiently explored. Viewed in the context of Fett's influence on conservation policy in Norway, Erling Viskjø's design for the two new government buildings can be seen in dialogue with Fett's principles of urban conservation.

Erling Viksjø and Harry Fett are considered to be on opposite sides of the debate that preceded the construction of a new government quarter and the demolition of the nineteenth-century listed hospital complex called Empirekvartalet designed by Christian Heinrich Grosch. Seemingly, Viksjø

Vestibyle, Erling Viksjø's
winning proposal of 1939

stands out as the winner, getting his modernist icons built, while Fett is
the loser unable to rescue Empirekvartalet from demolition. Looking closer,
the picture is less clear. Even though Fett retired in 1945 and his plea of
protection was overruled, his authority played out in other ways. His ideas
of urban conservation had struck root in the political and disciplinary
landscape, and they arguably changed the course of the government
building process.

The government buildings can be seen as the result of a negotiation
between two opposing "ideologies": *modernism* and *urban conservation*.
The two government buildings appear to be conceived according to the
first: solitary, freestanding buildings on pilotis, placed in a park, creating
a secure distance to the surrounding historic city. On a closer look, we see
that this modernist complex emerged in response to a dense configuration
of historical buildings.

In 1939, when working on the competition for a new government
quarter, Erling Viksjø was forced to confront the illusion of a Grand Master
Plan that always has haunted Oslo. A common (mis)conception is that the
city's planners and politicians never have managed to follow through with
a coherent plan, leaving behind a number of half-executed fragments: a
collage city of partly conflicting schemes. Nowhere was this more evident
than at Hammersborg in 1939: the apparent incoherency between the
placement and design of Trinity Church (1858), Deichmanske Library (1933),
the main fire station (1941), the Empirekvartalet (1807-26) and the old
government building (1906). One could argue that the inconsistent
ensemble represents a failure and a set of missed opportunities, but
alternatively you could name this condition a particular *Oslo-essence*,
reflecting distinct qualities and inherent principles of urban planning.
Arguably, Viksjø took this into consideration when designing a new
government quarter.

Looking into the process that led to the destruction of Empirekvartalet
and the construction of Høyblokka and Y-blokka, it becomes apparent
how much the idea of urban conservation evolved through negotiations
between new and old. The competition brief asked for projects that
respected the old government building from 1906, but neither the

Viksjø's proposal (left), and the proposal of the Antiquarian Building Committee (right)

governmental proposition that assigned the site nor the competition brief mentioned the old hospital quarter, treating its destruction as assumed. Forty-nine proposals were submitted, and in the spring of 1940 the jury selected four "winners," none of which was found entirely suitable. Three of five members of the jury found the site inappropriate for the program, not because it housed an ensemble of prominent, listed hospital buildings, but due to "its inability to site a contemporary, monumental and practical governmental building complex."[6] The jury report mentions the old hospital briefly, stating that some of the proposals allowed for the temporary keeping of the old hospital building until the government building was completed.

In 1946, when Viksjø's proposal finally was selected among the four winners of the 1939 competition, it was partly because it would allow for the Empirekvartalet to be preserved, a fact that helped maneuver the building project through the protest storm that would follow. The project, now relocated so it would fit between the existing hospital buildings and downscaled and downgraded to a "government office building," was only meant to be a temporary solution until a proper government building could be built. Erling Viksjø developed the project according to directions from the building committee, directions that implied the demolition of Empirekvartalet. The project was maneuvered "secretly" through the city council and the parliament without approval from either the Antiquarian Building Committee or the State Architect (equivalent to today's Statsbygg).

In 1949, a fierce public debate accelerated, becoming the first real preservation debate in Norway. The debate took place in the press and in public fora and included architects, antiquarians, politicians, writers, and prominent members of the "cultural elite." The debate among architects, well documented in *Byggekunst*,[7] the Norwegian journal of architecture, reflects a whole new attitude towards urban conservation. The uproar against the destruction of the Empirekvartalet was nearly unanimous, the opponents including the Antiquarian Building Committee, the State Architect, the Oslo regulation council, the editor of *Byggekunst*, and a row of prominent "modernist" architects such as Herman Munthe-Kaas, Gudolf Blakstad, Nicolai Beer, Knut Knutsen, Jens Selmer, and P.A.M. Mellbye.

Høyblokka placed among the existing hospital buildings, 1958

The Antiquarian Building Committee, led by the new Director General of the Directorate of Cultural Heritage (and Harry Fett's former right hand), Arne Nygård-Nilssen, presented an alternative proposal merging Erling Viksjø's project with the Empirekvartalet, preserving three of the four hospital buildings. The new building was centrally positioned on the northern façade of the Henrik Bull building and split in two angled wings when encountering the complex urban setting of Arne Garborgs plass. It is notable that the building took on the Y-shape that Viksjø would later pursue. The proposal was arguably not a convincing one, but in line with Harry Fett's (and Giovannoni's) ideas: inserting new functions into the existing urban fabric by partial demolition and by a reorientation of the urban space with a building of appropriate scale.

In response to public uproar, Viksjø developed a similar proposal in 1952 (now lost) that preserved some of the historical structures, among them a few of the hospital buildings and the allée of trees. The idea of a modernist, high-rise building threaded into the dense, historical urban fabric is quite radical, and most likely not in line with Viksjø's original intentions, but possibly inspired by (or governed by) the 1949 proposal of the Antiquarian Building Committee. The potential of this "urban conservation strategy" becomes apparent when contemplating photos of the newly completed Høyblokka still accompanied by all the hospital buildings.

Although the public debates certainly pushed Viksjø to alter his original scheme, his original proposal from 1939 already showed resonances with urban conservation strategies.

The positioning of the Høyblokka in his scheme echoed Stener Lenschow's initial design for the government quarter from 1891. His winning scheme (inherited and completed by Henrik Bull in 1906) had the form of a giant H that was destined to replace the entire hospital complex, but due to poor economy, only the southern "arm" of the building was completed. Viksjø not only performed the delicate balancing act of stepping among the existing buildings of Grosch, he also had to navigate in the haunted landscape of a project never realized. In Viksjø's many sketches, we can see how much attention he paid to the historical buildings of Grosch, Lenschow, and Bull. The perspective drawing from

Viksjø's sketch of Høyblokka as the backdrop of Trinity Church

the competition proposal of 1939 clearly reveals how the building is symmetrically placed on the Bull building, completing the center part of the never-realized H-shaped scheme of Lenschow. Unlike the final version, the buildings are attached, and Høyblokka can be understood as Viksjø's "take" on Bull. This is accentuated by the fact that the ground floor of the glass building is rusticated, imitating the granite façade of Bull's building and the rusticated ground floor of Grosch's hospital buildings. The symmetrical façade of Viksjø, which in the 1939 version is formulated as a vertical niche in the full height of the building, alludes to the iconic, symmetrically placed entrances of the hospital building of Grosch.

It seems like Viksjø was struggling with two conflicting strategies of urban conservation: one is to resurrect the ghostly H-scheme of Lenschow, the other to commemorate the formal garden within the hospital quarter. He dealt with this partly by preserving the Linden allée that connected the hospital building to Akersgaten, now framing the entrance of Høyblokka. The 1939 rusticated ground floor would later be replaced by an "open" floor supported by pilotis (with their own form of rustication in sandblasted concrete patterns), allowing the public to move through the building, similar to the 1943 Ministry of Education and Health building in Rio de Janeiro.

Viksjø's façade choices for the Høyblokka positioned it as a backdrop for the existing historical monuments. In the final scheme, the glass skin of 1939 was replaced by a load-bearing concrete façade. The windows are set deep in the façade, giving minimal reflection and arguably attracting less attention than a glass façade would have done. The freehand sketches of Viksjø clearly show how the façade is conceived as a grid background for the surrounding buildings, giving Trinity Church, Deichmanske Library, and the Bull building their required attention. Whether this achieved the desired effect or not, it shows how persistently he tried to incorporate the surrounding buildings in his scheme. Viksjø is employing a "strategy of disguise," partly by lifting the building off the ground, partly by veiling it in a deep gridded façade.

Viksjø's decision to replace the stone cladding with an unclad concrete structure can also be understood as a way to adapt to the historical setting, acknowledging the surrounding load-bearing masonry façades: the bare brick façades of Trinity Church and the fire station, the stone façade of the

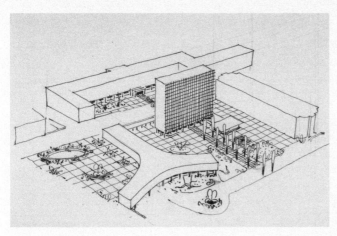

Erling Viksjø, Development of the government quarter, bird's-eye view, Akersgata, Oslo, 1958

Bull building, and the massive rustic foundations of Deichmanske Library. The *naturbetong*, invented by Viksjø and Sverre Jystad, a technique that by the use of sandblasting exposes the river-gravel aggregate of the concrete compound, turns the building into a mediator between historical and new building techniques.

The evolution of Y-blokka reveals a similar process of adjustment and response to historical context. The building appeared for the first time in a 1947 rendering in the shape of a small, one-story pavilion attached to Høyblokka. The building was small and obviously not born out of a need for more office space.

In 1952, it appeared as a freestanding, T-shaped, three-story building, not unlike the 1949 proposal from the Antiquarian Building Committee.

Arguably Viksjø was working according to the modernist convention of accompanying a vertical building with a horizontal one, in line with the 1952 UN building in New York, but there seem to be other strategies unfolding. The perspective drawings of the final version, following the inauguration of the Høyblokka in 1959, show the Y-blokka as a "framing device." On the one hand, the building divided Trinity Church and Deichmanske Library (whose designs were characterized by Viksjø as an unfortunate collision of styles[8]), and on the other hand it framed the views of passersby and established coherent urban spaces.

The decision to turn the building from a T into a Y is crucial: while the T created two concave corners and more static urban spaces, the Y ensured a continuous movement between the surrounding buildings. As a result, the building can be characterized as less a building than a mediator of existing urban spaces. Y-blokka, regarded by many as Viksjø's greatest invention, is a sort of non-monument, or at least a building that withdraws from the center stage, leaving it open to the other actors in play.

In hindsight, what apparently looks a collision of contradictory urban schemes reveals a deliberate and sophisticated strategy of urban conservation. Even though Erling Viksjø was under economic, political, and social pressure, and clearly was acting according to several design principles, he arguably was a practitioner of urban conservation. The influence of Harry Fett should not be underestimated: he gave fierce resistance to demolition

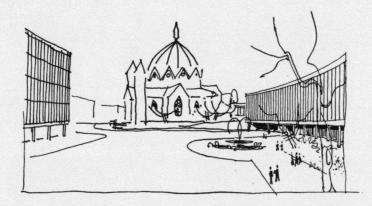

and thereby influenced public opinion, and most importantly, he constructed a conceptual framework for urban conservation that would allow for the development and growth of the contemporary city of Oslo.

One would expect that urban planners and architects involved in the current planning process for a new government quarter would immerse themselves in the history of Hammersborg and the underlying strategies of Harry Fett and Erling Viksjø. It has not happened, perhaps due to a lack of interest and expertise, or an inability to establish multidisciplinary forms of collaboration. Erling Viksjø's government quarter is a rare and early example of urban conservation of the twentieth century. Our task is to establish an *urban conservation utopia* for the twenty-first century, and the new government quarter is the perfect place to start.

## Notes

1   Francesco Bandarin and Ron van Oers, *The Historic Urban Landscape: Managing Heritage in an Urban Century* (Oxford: Wiley-Blackwell, 2012), vii–xxiv.

2   Françoise Choay, *The Invention of the Historic Monument* (New York: Cambridge University Press, 2001), 131.

3   Lucia Allais, "Will to War, Will to Art," in *Cultural Internationalism and the Modernist Aesthetics of Monuments, 1932–1964* (PhD diss., MIT, 2008), 65.

4   Harry Fett, Peter Glen, and Kristin B. Aavitsland, "Continuity (1949)," *Future Anterior* 7, no. 2 (2010): 34–37.

5   Kristin B. Aavitsland, *Harry Fett: historien er lengst* (Oslo: Pax, 2014).

6   Jury report, *Byggekunst* 22 (1940): 44.

7   *Byggekunst* 5 (1949).

8   Erling Viksjø, "Det nye regjeringsbygget," *Byggekunst* 1 (1959): 3.

Erik Langdalen is a Professor and the Head of the Institute of Form, Theory and History at the Oslo School of Architecture and Design.

Case Study

# Mediation and Preservation

## Mattias Ekman

When the car bomb exploded in the center of the Norwegian government quarter on July 22, 2011, immediately 50,000 square meters, or a third of the government's total office space, was rendered unusable. In addition to the shock of the bombing and the following massacre on Utøya island, the government faced the immediate relocation of several of its ministries and the task of initiating the process of rebuilding the government premises.

After the blast the most severely damaged buildings — the Høyblokka, the Y-blokka, the S-blokka, and the R4 — changed little in the first years to come, once the thousands of government documents spread all over the site had been salvaged and the debris cleared out. In contrast, the cultural perception of the buildings came to change dramatically, a process that started from the moment the first photographs of the devastated buildings appeared on news Web sites. The mediated images of the government

A newspaper page with a photograph taken on the roof terrace of the Høyblokka, typical of the period before the July 22nd bombing. China's Premier Zhao Ziyang visits Oslo and Prime Minister Kåre Willoch shows the view.

architecture in the weeks to come dramatically increased Norwegians' familiarity with the site and established it as a new national symbol. In the following it is argued that the mediation and following debate, rather than the bombing, altered the cultural status of the government buildings, suggesting that novel alternatives for preservation may arise as a result of dissemination of architectural imagery and public exchange of historic facts and symbolism.[1]

### Environmental image of the government quarter

With Kevin Lynch's seminal book *The Image of the City*, published in 1960, architects and planners were made aware that people hold mental representations of the environments they live in or know of.[2] Building on research by anthropologists, geographers, sociologists, and artists, he sketched up a theory and basic grammar for the constructs he termed *environmental images*, "the generalized mental picture of the exterior physical world that is held by an individual. The image is the product both of immediate sensation and of the memory of past experience, and it is used to interpret information and to guide action."[3] The environmental images should not be mistaken for two-dimensional visual memories of the environment. They are rather three-dimensional constructs in memory, abstracted and schematized, highlighting particular features and interrelations and employed for our orientation and way-finding.

Prior to the July 22nd bombing, many Oslo citizens had walked through the quarter on their way to the commercial city center, the city library, or one of the many churches in the area. People who worked for the government and thousands of others who had their workplace nearby would have the area's streets and landmarks standing out in their environmental image of Oslo. Most Norwegians also knew the quarter from political reportage in newspapers, on television, or on the Internet. Historical press photographs showed politicians posing in front of one of the buildings or prime ministers receiving foreign heads of state on the top floor of the Høyblokka, the most salient building.

By fusing repeated sensory impressions from visits or media into such spatial constructs of the mind, the individual becomes capable of

The Høyblokka on the front page of *Aftenposten* on July 23, 2011, the day after the bombing. The image of the building as a representative backdrop has been replaced by one of the architecture as victim in the mediation following July 22. Unusually for the newspaper, the page is devoid of any headlines, text, secondary images, or advertising.

orienting himself or herself in the environment. A spatial complex like that of the government quarter with several streets, façades, and interiors cannot be viewed from any one standpoint, and only by means of the environmental image is one able to handle the architectural interrelations.

### Disseminating architecture and transforming the image

Soon after the bomb went off, a torrent of photographs, videos, maps, graphics, and written and spoken descriptions of the devastated territory saturated national and international media. In Norway the exposure was extreme. A search made in the archive of the largest Norwegian press image distributor with the search term *regjeringskvartalet*, the common term for the quarter, produced 120 times as many photographs dated to the one-year period following July 22, 2011, compared to the year before.[4] A fifth of them, almost 2,500 pictures, were made available in the week after the bombing, which is more than one and a half times as many as those published in the preceding ten years.

Most television channels covered the event extensively. Shortly after the explosion, the Norwegian broadcasting company NRK started broadcasting a program that ran continuously for thirty-six hours.[5] A search on their Web site in November 2012 for the term *regjeringskvartalet* gave almost 5,000 hits.[6] Searches carried out in the Nordic media archive Retriever Research in the winter of 2012 to 2013 similarly illustrate the dramatic increase of the use of the term *regjeringskvartalet* in journalistic material. The occurrence of articles containing the term increased from almost 600 a year before to a little less than 9,000 in the year after, or more than fifteen times the frequency. The government quarter in Norwegians' environmental image was subject to strong influence in the time after July 22 — and it arguably underwent a radical transformation.

### Adding memories

One who had inspired Kevin Lynch's book was the French sociologist Maurice Halbwachs, with his writings on *collective memory* (*mémoire collective*).[7] What distinguishes Halbwachs' conceptualization of the spatial image in memory from those of his contemporaries is his emphasis of its support of other memory processes: one remembers the environment to better remember other things. Halbwachs' term *spatial framework of memory (cadre spatial de la mémoire)*, the counterpart to Lynch's environmental image, suggests a stable construct with particular features common to a social group. The individuals employ group-specific reference points in the spatial framework to structure their collective memory — social relations, group-historical events, codes of behavior, ethics, symbolism, etc. With Halbwachs' term we can appreciate how government officials would sustain a collective image of the quarter with detailed knowledge of streets and interiors through their daily interaction with the site. Also, we may recognize how Norwegian nationals shared an image of the government high rise because of its depiction in political reportage.

With the transformation of the spatial framework that followed the spread of images of the devastated buildings came new collective memories. For instance, the entrance to the high rise turned into an index of the van that carried the bomb and its aftermath. The quarter in people's spatial framework now seemed to cue emotionally disturbing memories. Employees of the government spoke out, saying that they could not move back into the same premises, as these would remind them of the bombing.[8] In the undamaged government building R6, the last of the three paintings forming the artwork *Lyset forsvinner — bare vi lukker øynene* (The light disappears — if we close our eyes), commissioned before the terror attack, was never installed.[9] The depiction of the government high rise next to papers flying in the air and what could appear as dead people gave the employees unwanted associations to the events of July 22.

### Disputing the memories
Parallel to the dissemination of images and eyewitness accounts a debate unfolded in the media about whether the buildings should be torn down or restored.[10] Arguing against a perceived threat of demolition, art and architecture historians, artists, architects, and conservators spoke about the symbolism of the architecture. Already in the first article of this genre, the government quarter was presented as the "center point for Norwegian nation building," the main site of political administration since

the city became the administrative seat of the Kingdom of Norway in 1814.[11] The first government building, the 1906 Gamleblokka, symbolized "the need of the state to mark a solid nation" at the time of the secession from the union with Sweden in 1905.[12] The Høyblokka and the Y-blokka, because of the unique concrete casting techniques and integrated sandblasted artwork signed by Pablo Picasso in collaboration with the Norwegian artist Carl Nesjar, should make us remember their position as the foremost exemplars of Norwegian modernist architecture and the country's contacts with the international art scene. The grid system of the façades should recall the development of social democracy after World War II, symbolizing equality and regularity.[13]

The debate saw authorized experts provide the general public with ready-made memories that would compete with those of terror or disinterest in the concrete architecture. They were attached to already canonized narratives of national history. The years 1814 and 1905 were brought forward, the most emblematic years in the historical chronology of modern Norway, also when the political processes of these years did not directly make an imprint on the architecture. The rhetorical gestures may be understood as an attempt to influence the memories bound to the quarter in the spatial framework of the general public. By letting the buildings attach themselves to important symbols in national history as well as international art history, they would be lent legitimacy that could save them from demolition.

### Reordering collective memory

Gradually media dissemination and the debate changed the image of the government quarter into one of a collection of heavily symbolic buildings. The rebuilding project became a delicate process of navigating different representations of the Norwegian nation and government. Administered by the government, its success or failure relies on public opinion. To give form to the quarter implies to give form to it as an associative construct in the spatial framework of Norwegians' memory.

This is the political and cultural context that architects and other consultants enter into. In addition to logistic, economic, and security-related choices, the future design of the site must contend with the memories that the public recalls: associations with terror, political history, architecture, and art history. In the planning of the new quarter several decisions lie out of reach of the architects and consultants. The government's decision to dispose of the two newest buildings, the R5 and R6, and tear down the Y-blokka, S-blokka, and R4, as well as to preserve the Høyblokka, Gamleblokka, and the only remaining nineteenth-century feature, a linden tree avenue in front of the high rise, was taken in May 2014 on the basis of two reports on the demarcation of the future quarter boundaries (KVU, KS1)[14] and one on preservation.[15] Architects may however accept or reject the premises of their tasks. In the parallel commission (*parallelloppdrag*) for ideas towards a state-controlled zoning plan (*statlig reguleringsplan*), which ended in April 2015, the student team from the Oslo School of Architecture and Design proposed to preserve the Y-blokka, against the directions given, but this advice was not followed in the subsequent recommendation of urban form principles by the client Statsbygg.[16]

Decisions regarding the preservation of buildings in the process following the July 22nd bombing, it has been argued here, were not left to the architects and consultants of the two reports and the parallel commission. Rather, they were made by the government on the basis of their expertise and the public debate, and ultimately the extensive mediation of imagery of the government quarter. Arguably, it is as a result of the strengthening of the spatial framework of the quarter among Norwegians and its new associations with nodes in political history and architecture history that the politicians of two subsequent governments have needed to propose the preservation of the Høyblokka, the Gamleblokka, and the linden avenue and the demolition of the S-blokka, R4, and the Y-blokka. As a result of the bombing in the government quarter, the former buildings have become much more well known by Norwegians, and the memories attached to them have been raised to the level of a national symbol by the debaters. Such dramatic changes to the public's perception are not easily ignored by an elected government. It is in this reordering of national collective memory that one should search for the reasons for preservation.

## Notes

1    This chapter is mainly based on the doctoral thesis Mattias Ekman, "Edifices: Architecture and the Spatial Frameworks of Memory" (PhD thesis, Oslo School of Architecture and Design, 2013), esp. ch. 6, 237–312.

2    Kevin Lynch, *The Image of the City* (Cambridge: MIT Press, 1960).

3    Ibid., 4. On Lynch's theoretical background and the influences on his thinking, see ibid., appendix A, 123–39; Ekman, "Edifices," 136–49; Kirsten Wagner, "Die visuelle Ordnung der Stadt: Das Bild der Stadt bei Kevin Lynch," in *Räume der Stadt: Von der Antike bis heute*, ed. Cornelia Jöchner (Berlin: Reimer, 2008), 317–33.

4    Search carried out November 7, 2012, on http://www.scanpix.no.

5    Alexandra Bech Gjørv et al., "Rapport fra 22. juli-kommisjonen," NOU 2012:14 (Govt. report, 2012), 22, accessed October 19, 2015, https://www.regjeringen.no/no/dokumenter/nou-2012-14/id697260/.

6    Search carried out November 6, 2012, on http://www.nrk.no.

7    Maurice Halbwachs, *The Collective Memory*, trans. Francis J. Ditter Jr. and Vida Yazdi Ditter (New York: Harper & Row, 1980) [Fr. orig. (1950). On Halbwachs' influence on Lynch, see Ekman, "Edifices," 145–46, 53–55. Halbwachs' term "collective memory" would later enter into the architectural vocabulary through Aldo Rossi's use of it. Aldo Rossi, *The Architecture of the City*, trans. Diane Ghirardo and Joan Ockman, 1st Amer. ed. (Cambridge: Opposition books/MIT Press, 1982) [It. orig., 4th ed. (1978)], 130.

8    Jorun Sofie F. Aartun, "Tanken på å vende tilbake på jobb i tiende etasje gir meg fysisk ubehag," *Dagens Næringsliv*, October 13, 2011, 28.

9    "R6, Government Building," KORO Public Art Norway, accessed October 8, 2015, http://publicartnorway.org/prosjekter/r6-government-building/.

10    For a detailed analysis of the debate, see Ekman, "Edifices," 272–78, 89–94.

11    Architecture historian and former director of Oslo Museum Lars Roede, quoted in Kjersti Nipen, "Bygningene formet det nye Norge," *Aftenposten Morgen*, July 25, 2011, Kultur, 6. My translation.

12    Ibid. My translation.

13    Nina Berre, architecture historian and director of architecture at the National Museum, referenced in ibid.

14    Gaute Zakariassen and Ellen Viseth, "Har bestemt seg for å bevare Høyblokka," *NRK*, May 25, 2014, accessed October 9, 2015, http://www.nrk.no/norge/hoyblokka-bevares-_-y-blokka-rives-1.11738969; OPAK, Metier, and LPO arkitekter, "Konseptvalgutredning for fremtidig regjeringskvartal: Rapport til Fornyings-, administrasjons- og kirkedepartementet" (Govt. report, 2013), accessed October 19, 2015, https://www.regjeringen.no/globalassets/upload/fad/vedlegg/bst/konseptvalgsutredningen_rkv.pdf; Dovre Group and Transportøkonomisk institutt, "Fremtidig regjeringskvartal: Kvalitetssikring av beslutningsunderlag for konseptvalg (KS1). Rapport til Finansdepartementet og Kommunal- og moderniseringsdepartementet" (Govt. report, 2014), accessed October 19, 2015, https://www.regjeringen.no/globalassets/upload/KMD/BST/RKV/KS1FremtidigRegjeringskvartal.pdf.

15    Riksantikvaren, "Regjeringskvartalet: Riksantikvarens utredning om verneverdi og ny bruk" (Govt. report, 2013), accessed October 19, 2015, http://hdl.handle.net/11250/176847.

16    Bryony Roberts et al., "Åpent kvartal/Open Quarter: Parallelloppdrag" (April 12, 2015), accessed October 9, 2015, http://www.statsbygg.no/files/prosjekter/RKVnytt/parallelloppdragene/aho/ahoParallelloppdrag.pdf; Statsbygg, "Nytt regjeringskvartal: Statsbyggs anbefaling til byformprinsipp for nytt regjeringskvartal" (October 5, 2015), accessed October 9, 2015, http://www.statsbygg.no/Files/prosjekter/RKVnytt/anbefaling/anbefRKVplansjer.pdf.

Mattias Ekman is a postdoctoral fellow at the Department of Culture Studies and Oriental Languages at the University of Oslo, and holds a PhD from the Oslo School of Architecture and Design.

Case Study

# Site Images

The following images represent the many historical phases of the government quarter. Maps illustrate the changes to the site over time, and historical photographs depict the modernist structures of Norwegian architect Erling Viksjø — the Høyblokka and the Y-blokka buildings.

Documenting the changes to the site after the attack on July 22, 2011, photographs reveal the damage and maps represent the plans for future development in the government quarter. These plans formed the foundation for the planning process, in which the AHO and GSAPP Team participated.

Main political and religious monuments in Oslo in 1794

Main political and religious monuments in Oslo in 1900

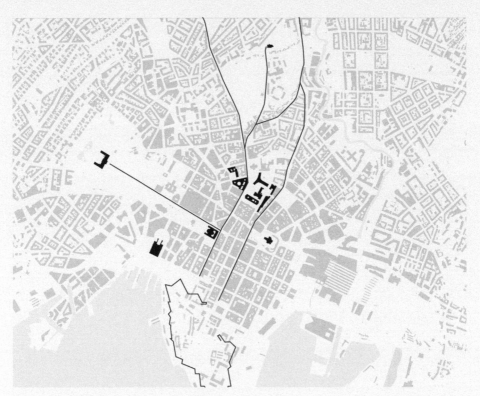

Main political and religious monuments in Oslo in 2014

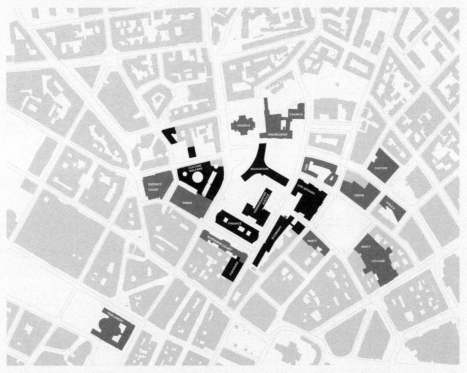

Government quarter in 2014, with buildings for ministry offices, press, unions, courts, police, and other functions

Monumental Field of
Government Quarter, 2014

**A.** Trinity Church, Alexis
de Chateauneuf, 1858

**B.** Y-blokka, Erling Viksjø, 1969

**C.** Høyblokka, Erling Viksjø,
1958

**D.** Gamleblokka, Henrik Bull
and Stener Lenschow, 1906

**E.** Møllergata 19, Jacob Wilhelm
Nordan, 1866

**F.** Fire station, Eystein
Michalsen, 1939

**G.** Deichmanske Library,
Nils Olaf Reiersen, 1933

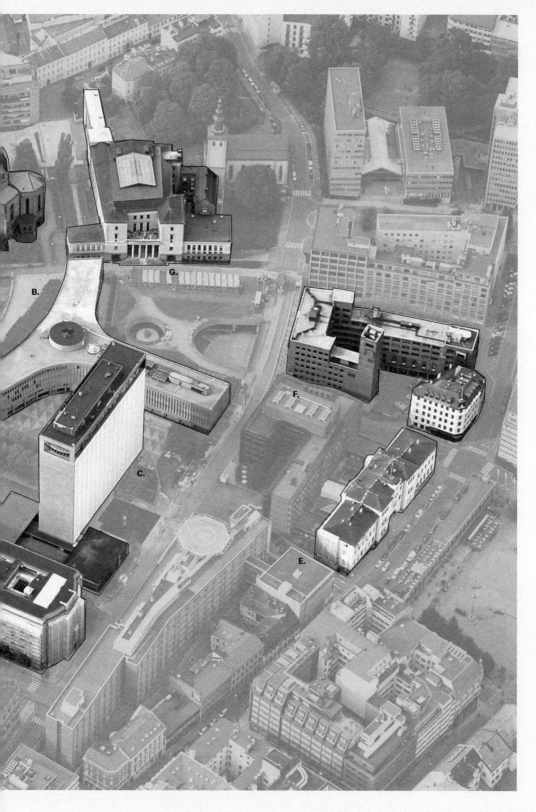

Høyblokka, Oslo, 1958–59

Høyblokka, Oslo, 1958–59

Høyblokka at the end of a workday, 1962

Høyblokka, Oslo, 1958

Stairwell, Y-blokka, Oslo

Sandblasted image by Pablo Picasso, Y-blokka, Oslo

Høyblokka after the attack by Anders Breivik on July 22, 2011

Interior of Høyblokka cleared out after damage

Government quarter before attack on July 22, 2011

Government plan "Konsept Øst" from 2013, proposing demolition of Y-blokka and concentration of new ministry offices in towers next to the Høyblokka

Government demolition decisions after attack

■ Buildings being demolished

■ Buildings being preserved

# Open Quarter Master Plan

## AHO and GSAPP Team

**Team leader: Bryony Roberts; Critics: Erik Langdalen and Jorge Otero-Pailos; GSAPP teacher: Craig Konyk**
PhD Advisers: Christian Parreno, Guttorm Ruud; AHO students: Helle Bendixen, Nina Gjersoe, Liv Hanstad, Hauk Lien, Eva Negård, Ida Nordstrøm, Liv Oppebøen, Rebecca Schulz; GSAPP students: Paridhi Agarwal, Stephanie Jones, Wesley LeForce, Michael Middleton, Andre Stiles

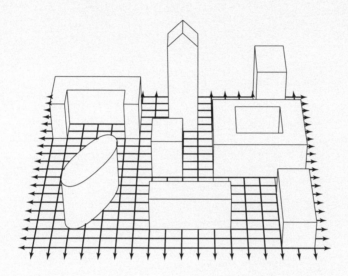

Arguing for the integration of historical architecture and new construction in the government quarter, the collaborative team from the Oslo School of Architecture and Columbia GSAPP focused on transforming the ground plane. The existing site is an unusually diverse monumental field, which represents government authority through a multiplicity of insitutions. The Open Quarter project aims to enhance and extend this monumental field, through a thickened ground plane that grows from the existing spatial grid, to offer improved circulation, additional office space, and garden atriums.

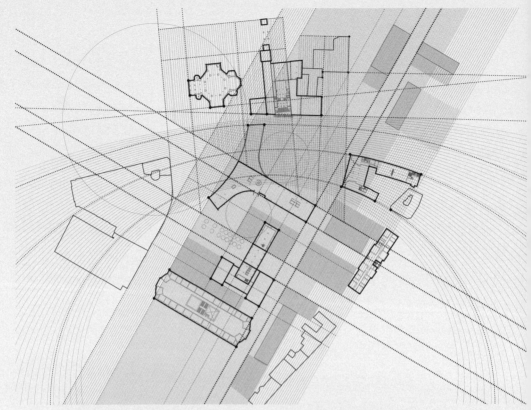

Analytical plan showing the existing lines of the site and the placement of new towers and gardens. In the existing site condition, the lines of the modernist Y-blokka and Høyblokka connect the edges of the other monuments, creating a network of enclosed public spaces. Continuing this logic, the new construction extends the existing lines to guide the distribution of new towers and public spaces. The composition leaves room around the historical monuments, and frames them with sunken gardens and light wells. The new, thickened ground plane produces east-west and north-south connections, enabling better pedestrian connections across the site, and opens the site to the surrounding city.

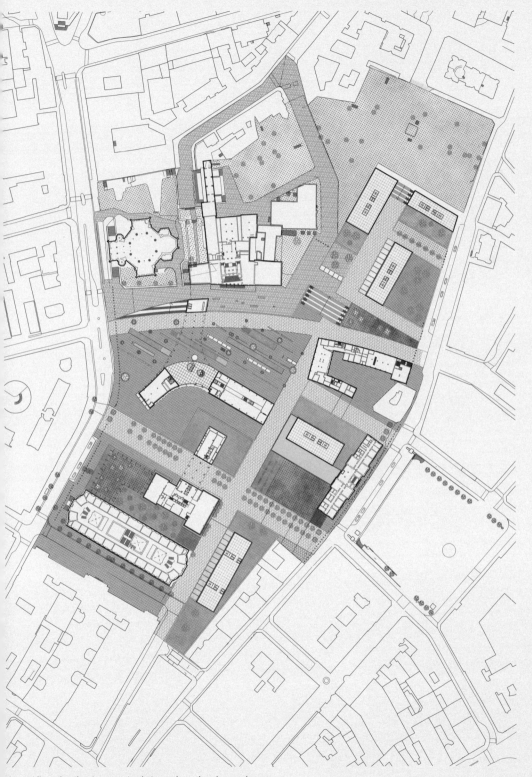

Ground floor plan showing new circulation paths and sunken gardens

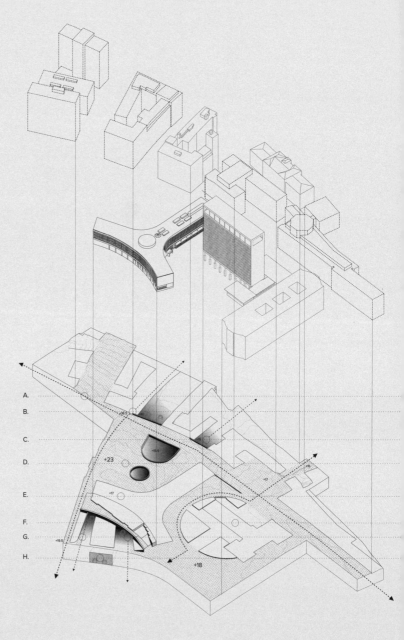

**A.** Grubbegata will work as a link between north and south, and connect to the existing green areas.

**B.** In today's situation, the connection has been broken, with a covered staircase between Grubbegata and Hammersborggata. By closing off the exit ramps to Ring 1, and then lowering Ring 1 to the same level as it is on either side of the existing ramps, we are able to establish a new continuous ground level.

**C.** In the existing situation, the pedestrian path between east and west runs by a highly trafficked road under the lid. The passage is experienced as dark, noisy, and unsafe. By removing the lid and lowering Ring 1, we bring new life into Arne Garborgs plass.

**D.** Arne Garborgs plass is redefined as a car-free city space at the same level as the square in front of the Høyblokka. The area between Deichmanske Library and Arne Garborgs plass becomes a new cultural programming zone that brings activity into the site.

**E.** In today's situation, the Y-blokka is a barrier to east-west movement. Removing the lid above Arne Garborgs plass creates a free passage under the north wing of the Y-blokka, breaking down this barrier. By doing this, we also create more passages between east and west which activates the area, and creates movement through it.

**E.** The passage through the Høyblokka is restored as a connection between east and west.

**F.** The entry ramps to the ring-road are removed.

**G.** Today Ring 1 is curved upwards and meets the entry ramps by Arne Garborgs plass. By removing the entry ramps and lowering the ring-road to an adjoining level, Arne Garborgs plass will become car-free.

Before

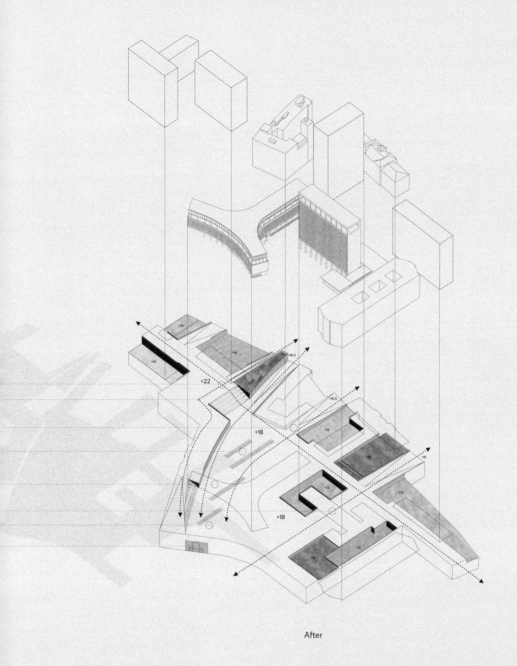

After

Oslo skyline, showing towers following the government phasing plan for 115,000 square meters of office space by 2034, and 62,500 additional square meters of office space by 2064

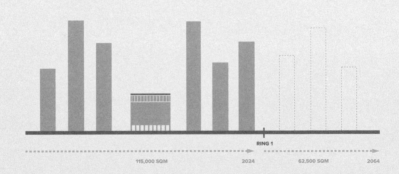

115,000 SQM      2024      RING 1      62,500 SQM      2064

Oslo skyline, showing towers as proposed in Open Quarter, which maintain the scale of the Høyblokka and preserve the Y-blokka, but meet the same area demands by changing the phasing of construction and thickening the ground plane

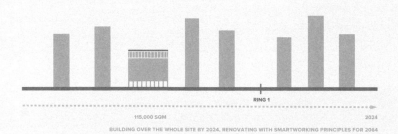

RING 1

115,000 SQM — 2024

BUILDING OVER THE WHOLE SITE BY 2024, RENOVATING WITH SMARTWORKING PRINCIPLES FOR 2064

SPACE BELOW GROUND

View of Open Quarter master plan, showing connection from Youngstorget across the site

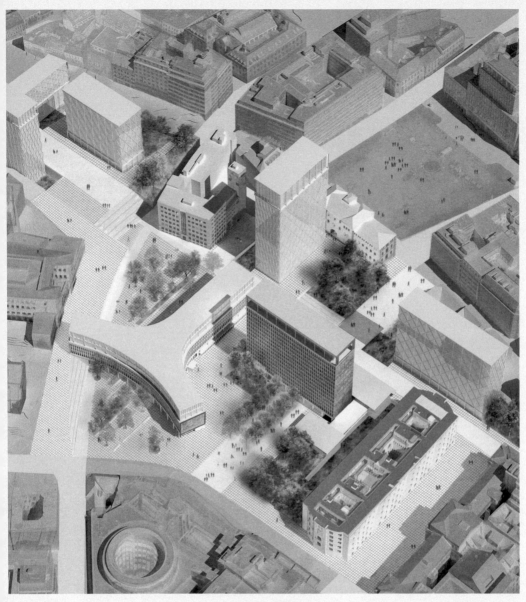

Aerial view of Open Quarter master plan, showing five new towers that echo Høyblokka

Section cut through the Y-blokka, showing movement in the east-west direction

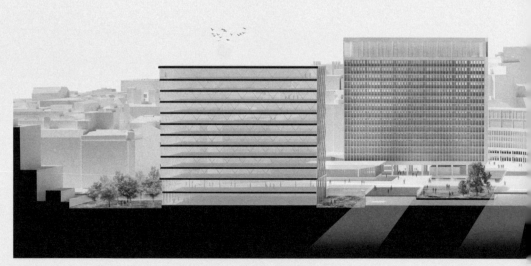

Section cut in the north-south direction, showing integration of gardens and towers

View of Arne Garborgs plass, showing the new pedestrian connection from east to west and the nexus
of cultural programming between the restored Y-blokka and Deichmanske Library

View of the memorial to July 22, 2011, in the arm of the Y-blokka that extends towards Deichmanske Library

View of the Høyblokka
building, with restored
pedestrian access under
the tower, as it was
originally designed

Case Study: AHO Team Project

**Nine Points Towards an Expanded Notion of Architectural Work**
Thordis Arrhenius

**Pedagogy Roundtable**
Thordis Arrhenius, Jorge Otero-Pailos, Erik Langdalen, and Bryony Roberts

**Teaching Bibliography**
Bryony Roberts

# Pedagogy

# Nine Points Towards an Expanded Notion

## of Architectural Work

## Thordis Arrhenius

## 1. Alteration

In postindustrial societies, clusters of problems in the built environment revolve around the question of how to reuse and alter the already there — the "existing." There is an urgent and obvious sustainable significance in alteration, at the level of urban resilience, urban identity, and sustainability. A central effect of global capitalism, evident in postindustrial Europe, is the production of derelict spaces and spatial structures that have lost their use because of changing urban patterns and economics; what to do with "all this" is of pressing concern. But the issue of alteration is also increasingly pressing in the dense built-up areas of the traditional city, or in the more recent manifestations of post-planning sprawl, where new technical or infrastructural demands constantly transform and adapt the existing. Under the name of urban regeneration, densification, modernization, retrofitting, reuse, or just preservation, building stock is constantly changed physically, technically, programmatically, and culturally.

In this situation, architects' core activities are increasingly concerned with alteration. Indeed, alteration is becoming one of the main tasks of architectural production. But in stark contrast, educational practice and the building industry are still mortgaged to the logic of new construction. Architecture is still defined generally in terms of the construction of new forms. Its identification as a discipline rests on associations tied to original intention and authorship, ideas that are complicated by the issue of alteration. The situation calls for a fundamental rethinking of the role of alteration in the discipline of architecture on all levels, from education and historical interpretation to factual implementation. As of now, no "theory" of alteration as a central condition of architectural practice exists. This suggests an urgent need to establish a new field of architectural research and pedagogy.

### 2. As Found

Theories and methods relating to the existing tend to be predicated on concepts inherent in preservation; discourses and practices that ultimately build on the notion of stasis and completion. Yet forces of change are always at stake in any restoration project, even when the stated objective is to preserve in its totality the built structure or environment, singled out as an object of conservation. To find a new pedagogy for alteration beyond stasis, it is necessary to explore processes of working with the existing in relation to change. To interact with the historical "as found," as a resource and a material for alteration, requires taking into consideration the processes that drive the conservation of the built environment, such as experiential economy, ecologies of reuse, social expectation, and mediation of the heritage object.

### 3. Site Specific

With this aim, a pedagogy of alteration works to identify site-specific qualities — material, spatial, and organizational — that reveal different aspects of the existing fabric and its spaces, uses, and histories. A crucial aspect of alteration is its relation to the specific (in contrast to the generic), calling for design innovations that consider the site as a driving force for change. This suggests a need to deepen and explore our knowledge of the existing on all levels, from the technical and economic to the historical and cultural. As well as grasping the specificity of the physical object, a crucial activity is to to map the forces of cultural expectation present in its various representations and mediations. How has the object been described and debated in the public press, for example? Which are the common popular narratives and rumors circulating around it? And how have these "non-authorized stories" been transcribed and reflected in the use and understanding of the building both as a physical "fact" and as a cultural artifact constructed over time? Here the notions of memory and agency in relation to the built object become important — how the building functions as a framework for memory, and, taking memory as an emotive force capable of moving individuals, the agency this functioning implies.

### 4. Medium

This wider understanding of the building as a mediation of different desires, functions, and politics introduces an important methodological issue. Traditionally, the physical building has occupied a privileged position in preservation. One aim of a pedagogy of alteration is to rethink this hierarchy. The "as-found" object here is understood as an entity that incorporates its own discourse and embraces the ideas, thoughts, and traditions that generate its shifting cultural meaning over time. An analysis of this "object" includes, as well as its physical materiality and spatial configuration, media and representations from different contexts that have constructed the meaning of the object — users, authors, economic and cultural values, and historical interpretation, as well as metaphors, assertions, and prejudices.

### 5. Mapping

The mapping process therefore has to be an inclusive, non-hierarchical activity in which everything related to the building/site is collected, organized, and considered on an equal level. In this task, the documentation tools developed in the field of architectural preservation and building archaeology are highly valid. However, alongside these quasi-objective methods, it is also necessary to include the register of the subjective — the individual meeting with an object, including vested interests and personal passions. At the center of such subjective and selective processes are positions of aesthetic judgment, which constitute an increasingly important although highly complex aspect of alteration.

### 6. Critical

An overarching aim of this research is to formulate and test strategies of using alteration to critically reframe the historical. The term "critical" is adopted here in a twofold sense: both as a method of self-reflection, interrogating one's own working methods and design choices, and also in the sense of scrutinizing an authorized body of knowledge, by challenging values and assumptions in the field of preservation. The confrontation of established preservation methods with techniques of change and alteration offers methods to rethink the notions of permanence within preservation and to reframe the obsession with the new in architecture. Taken together, these experiments in mapping and design processes provide resources for alteration that challenge conventional courses of action in both preservation and architecture. They allow sensitivity for material qualities and possibilities of the existing to be put to creative use, opening a dialogue with the past based on recognition rather than representation.

### 7. Fragment

As a result of engaging in these open processes, projects within the field of preservation are not necessarily complete in the modernistic sense that they claim to solve problems in their totality. Instead, they represent various scales of alteration, from internal spaces, through the interface between outside and inside, to the larger urban context and the design of change itself. The emphasis is then to use design as an analytical tool to develop and test out strategies, sensibilities, and attitudes concerning the existing. Taken together, these fragmentary projects relate critically to the history and practice of preservation by using the borders and limitations of preservation as a device to reframe the architectural monument, highlighting the notions of process and mutability over those of completion and permanence.

### 8. Pedagogical Devices

On another level, the work with alteration poses challenges to the paradigmatic values of architectural and preservation education. In architectural pedagogies, the dominance of concepts such as originality, authorship, and oeuvre is longstanding. Architecture's history developed as a sequential account of "authors" and their "works," and these concepts, inherited from the Beaux-Arts and the Bauhaus, continue to organize the disciplinary education of architects today. Embedded and hidden in the evaluation system, in cultures of judgment, such preoccupations relate architecture finally to the representation of individual new "works" and identify merit in the student through the judgment of those representations. If architectural education still indulges the image of the artist inventing in a realm of freedom and creativity, in cases of alteration this situation is reversed, if not less creative. The building is *there* and the architect is inventing in, on, or between existing structures, suggesting an altered relationship to the notion of the "work."

### 9. Architectural History

Finally therefore, working with alteration as a pedagogical device suggests a rethinking of the role of architectural history in architectural pedagogies. At a fundamental level, the discipline of architectural history is structured around how human intent is linked to the realization of discrete physical objects and must, in order to maintain its integrity, preserve its objects in all their materiality to prove and maintain the authored intent as *authentic*. Indeed, this constructed relation between materiality and authorship has constituted the binding link between architectural history and preservation — it is hard to imagine a discourse of preservation without one of architectural history. On the other hand, as a field of architectural inquiry and practice, alteration opens up a fundamental redefinition of architecture as a discipline that challenges authorship, intention, and oeuvre.

Thordis Arrhenius is a Professor of Cultural Heritage at Linköping University, and a former Professor at the Oslo School of Architecture and Design.

# Pedagogy Roundtable

## Thordis Arrhenius,
## Erik Langdalen,
## Jorge Otero-Pailos,
## and Bryony Roberts

<u>Culture</u>

**Bryony:** You all come from different institutions and experiences, but are working together to develop pedagogical ideas for preservation, in part through exchanges between the Oslo School of Architecture and Design (AHO) and the Columbia University Graduate School of Architecture, Planning and Preservation (GSAPP). You all teach a combination of design studios and seminars, working on the dialogue between design methods and contemporary preservation theory.

I wanted to hear your thoughts on teaching new methods of engaging existing buildings, specifically what tools you feel are urgent today. It seems that to develop visionary work in this field requires developing new tools of analysis, design, and representation, and also a new set of precedents. So to begin, Jorge, I'm curious to hear what kind of tools of analysis and of design you work on in your courses.

**Jorge:** Big data is informing new analytical tools in design practice. There is the smart city phenomenon of seeing the city as something to be constantly monitored and sensed and fed back onto itself and visualized.

But what happens with big data derived tools is that they tend to miss the things that can't be easily quantifiable as data. They can easily capture fast changes in the location of a car or a person, but they miss long changes over time, for example like those that buildings undergo. They also are less adequate for analyzing questions of cultural value or even politics, for analyzing the web of associations that help us understand buildings as parts of our lives, that make architecture a cultural object as opposed to just a functional tool. In other words, such data analytics are not able to grasp some of the research issues that the disciplines of architecture, preservation, and history have been most invested in. So I think we do have a challenge there, but there is also an opportunity to rethink what big data is and to rethink how we teach preservation in light of the inevitability of this huge digital transformation in how we document and think of the built environment.

**Bryony:** How do you think that more intangible information should be gathered? Is it there a subjective route and then maybe an intersubjective route in terms of how you gather social history? What do you tend to employ with your students?

**Jorge:** It depends what you mean by intersubjective. One could think of intersubjectivity as shared prejudices, in the best sense of the word — in Gadamer's sense, as what comes before judgment, something we refer to in shorthand with the word "culture." As preservationists, architects, artists we think of ourselves as cultural producers. Culture is not something we take for granted, but rather something we are committed to. I think that what's important is to help students articulate how they make commitments outside of themselves. What I see happening is students becoming interested in preservation and in analyzing existing buildings in order to find those commitments out there already, shared by others. They are able to say, "Well, in this building, for example, public housing from the 1930s, one can find a commitment to housing the middle class, the working class." Then they can ask: "Where is that today?" And maybe they'll find this is something really important to them. Something they want to commit to. Working on existing buildings offers an opportunity to be critical of contemporary culture, to commit to the pursuit of a different possible future.

**Bryony:** Thordis, you wrote about something similar in your text on pedagogy, where you describe gathering a spread of information beyond existing hierarchies, to obtain factual, personal, and political material. You suggested almost overwhelming yourself and your students with the data and the information in the beginning in order to see all aspects of the object. Can you talk a little bit about that?

**Thordis:** Yes, one strategy is clearly big data, or let's say scientific archaeology, where we believe in the possibility of accumulating all the "facts" and then acting. However, my experience is that this pseudo objectivity also creates, in some sense, a productive lack, or desire. Two-thirds into the term, the students start getting very nervous that they do not have their own project, but just data or facts. The challenge is not just how to accumulate all this information, but how to make it their own.

I remember one year we worked with trying to find another meditation of the object beyond facts and data. That is very hard to formulate in words or theories, but it's a way to act on the object, to love the object, to meet the object, to care for it. Here there is a whole field within preservation, and also a history (just think of Ruskin and his obsessive mapping of Venice) that is highly experimental in terms of redefining the object of preservation.

### Analysis

**Bryony:** To what degree do you think phenomenology comes in as a technique for understanding those other dimensions of a building? How do you all integrate that or not into that form of analysis?

**Jorge:** The old school architectural phenomenology studio teaching seems to be over. I don't see a lot of that in studios anymore. What I do see, maybe as the flip side, is the total absence of any discussion of architectural experience. Very seldom do people talk about the articulation of a space, the qualities of the space. So I think when people work with existing buildings, all of a sudden they are confronted with the richness of the experience, which can be overwhelming if you have not been trained to analyze it systematically, and it even paralyzes a designer. As Thordis was saying, it creates a type of anxiety, because students are now taught to represent buildings at a sort of mid-scale, from across the street, at an angle, in a perspective view, for example.

**Bryony:** Erik, this ties into some issues we talked about in relation to your last studio at AHO, which focused on postwar concrete architecture in

Oslo. One issue that came up was student anxiety about not being original and the confrontation with conventional notions of authorship. How do you deal with that as a teacher? And in terms of design tools, how do you approach teaching the design of interventions, which can sometimes be very intangible or piecemeal?

**Erik:** What I find interesting is not only the role of the teacher, but also how the pedagogy of architecture schools is on display when you teach preservation studios. Since we don't have a separate preservation program at AHO, we are part of the architectural program; all the students we get are trained as architects. When they enter preservation studios, they don't have the tools required. The students master the conventional tools of the architecture, but they run into trouble with preservation. And of course we also run into trouble as teachers, so we have to invent a new pedagogy along the way. Having preservation imbedded into the architecture program represents a great potential, enabling a merging of the two fields and moving preservation into the core of architecture.

In the concrete studio we focused on the working tools of the 1960s, when these buildings were conceived. I think one of the most wonderful moments during the semester was when the students started to replicate and develop the tools from the architects. That made the Preservation Studio not only about preservation of buildings, but also a preservation discourse about techniques and methods.

### Design Tools

**Bryony:** I want to push on what you said, because I think one of the questions for this type of work is — do you have to invent new tools for drawing, either for documenting or for designing intervention? I think one strategy that I see in practice, as with Mansilla + Tuñon in Spain, is that they tried to invent drawing techniques to show interstitial changes to existing buildings. The challenge is often how to show piecemeal alterations that convert disparate pieces into a new whole. But then there's another model, which you were just describing, where you actually appropriate techniques of a past time period. I'm wondering, are the drawing techniques of the 1960s actually the best ones to use in that scenario? What's the question that's being explored in remaking those drawings?

**Jorge:** It seems to me that the tools have been invented. That is to say, we just had a major digital revolution in how architects build up their designs. Most students don't have the experience, for example, of how architects until the twentieth century built up a façade design through layers upon layers of trace paper, each with a small modification. The break with the past is more profound than that of modernism. Modernists were still designing façades with the same drawing tools as their contemporary Beaux-Arts architects. Now students don't start with 2-D drawings (plans, sections, or façades); they start immediately with a 3-D model. This way of conceptualizing a design project is different in the mind. It doesn't require the type of section-plan relationship that one used to fuss about when building up a design through a series of 2-D drawings. So, when they look at an old building like Andrea Palladio's S. Giorgio Maggiore that has, for example, three or four façades composited together in one, they have difficulty engaging it. It's not that they can't understand, but they can't engage the process of that design in the same way, because their tools are different. So, I think that starting to draw again like in the Renaissance doesn't make any sense. That's not to say that such reenactments don't have value in themselves. They can be a form of historical research that may reveal important information about the process of design. But I think one has to now use the digital revolution, the digital tools, to try to then figure out a way to help students understand the design of historic buildings in a way that is relevant to them today.

**Thordis:** I totally agree. I think the new tools are essential. The whole development of scanning and documenting buildings three-dimensionally and also in moving images is crucial in providing new tools of understanding the existing.

One thing I think is extremely interesting in preservation is the challenge of actually understanding the physical matter of a building. How much does it weigh? What volume does it take? How much material has gone into the building? So you move from the very abstract in the drawing into the very concrete of the existing.

**Bryony:** That gets to the specific versus general theme that you brought up in your text on pedagogy. To me, the limitation of the representational techniques and design techniques that architects are taught in school is how much they remain at the level of the generic and the abstract. In general, in architecture, there's a lack of tools available to actually gather information about the specifics of the existing. Laser scanning, photogrammetry, they're all becoming more prevalent, but those have not yet become assimilated into the design process in a very easy way, so we still aren't used to dealing with the very specific information you can get from that.

**Thordis:** Yes, the new technology does move toward the specific much more. Scanning, for example, gets very clinical about the material, in a very different way from the early computer work. I think that comes closer to medicine and to anatomical drawings.

**Bryony:** It does give you a more corporeal, almost abject, experience of a building than plans, sections, and elevations.

**Erik:** It would be interesting to discuss what tools we need in preservation practice that are different from architectural practice, and in particular what tools are urgent. Scanning, for example, makes it much easier to survey a building, and mastering these tools can give preservation architects an advantage in the building process. I also wonder how long these will be two different disciplines; if architecture is one discipline and preservation is another, or if they are becoming one.

### Creativity

**Bryony:** Jorge, what do you think about that, being in a school with a distinct preservation department? Are architecture and preservation still separate disciplines?

**Jorge:** They're two related bodies of knowledge and related practices, and there's a lot of movement back and forth. I think the question at the core is, what is relevant knowledge in both of these fields? Preservation is very related to planning and to chemistry and to other disciplines. Architecture thinks of itself as a design discipline, and everything else is subservient to the notion of design.

So, the stakes are how to redefine design. I think that in preservation there is less emphasis on the question of design as the central articulating concept of the field. I would like to think that that's an opportunity to actually rethink related issues, like for example the notion of creativity. What constitutes creativity in preservation is not necessarily the same as what constitutes creativity within architecture.

It's difficult, because when you choose a field, you choose it because in a sense, it matches what you enjoy. A lot of students that come into architecture come because they would like to be designers. I think people who come into preservation do not necessarily come with the hopes of becoming designers, but they are creative practitioners. They come in with a desire to engage with culturally significant objects in a meaningful way and to help to protect them. So I think that the role of the academic experience is to satisfy those expectations, but also to open them up to deeper fundamental questions of the disciplines.

And so for me the stakes are, how do we begin to talk about creativity within a preservation program in relation to chemistry and planning and architecture and their different definitions of practice. That's where preservation participates in a larger cultural transformation of the understanding of creativity that we're in the midst of, partly because of this technological revolution.

**Bryony:** And how would you describe that creativity that would be specific to the preservation department?

**Thordis:** I could jump in here. I would say that it's alchemy rather than chemistry. The simplified idea of architecture is that it's about creating gifts. The architect draws us a building and it's a gift, to the client, to the users. And I think what is interesting about preservation is that it takes something existing and turns that into a gift. Something that is undervalued is given value. So it's not just that preservationists deal with objects out there that are historically significant. Often they also identify things and turn them into historical significant things.

**Bryony:** Jorge, would that be that the same as what you were picturing?

**Jorge:** That's definitely a big part of preservation, and one of the thrills is to find something that has been forgotten and to bring it back to the present, or as a present, a gift if you will. On the more pecuniary side, it becomes the real estate developer's mantra of repositioning assets, taking a distressed asset and making it a valuable asset. On the cultural side of things, it becomes the more historiographical question of finding what hasn't been studied yet, the missing pieces of the discipline, and making a contribution to knowledge by identifying something that has been forgotten or lost. So we have that full range there in preservation, and I think that as you move across that spectrum, the tools of preservation vary. They're moving from financial analysis to historiographical analysis, but in the end they're dealing with questions of value.

**Thordis:** Yes, the difference between the disciplines is that in preservation it's about identifying values in the already existing, while in architecture those values are assumed. So it's a form of alchemy, of turning dust into gold.

**Bryony:** There is also a whole range of aesthetic choices to be made as well. That is what most closely resembles design practice but then also diverges from it. There are moments of guesswork or approximation in which a choice has to be made, about color or the material resemblance of new pieces in comparison with old pieces. It's adding a foreign design, but one that is so relational and so responsive that it can never stand on its own as an object. That's the kind of design that is often hardest to pitch to architectural students as being a worthwhile form of authorship.

But in terms of that question of alchemy, it made me think of the fact that many of the studios we have taught in the last few years have taken on sites that were incredibly charged politically and culturally. I'm thinking of the Re-Store studios that you taught, Thordis, at AHO, and the last two studios you taught at Columbia, Jorge, and the government project in Oslo, which I taught last year. They're all dealing with very big-name sites. It seems to me that's an intentional choice to address the political dimension of preservation, but I wanted to hear from all of you about those choices. Also, I'm wondering whether the more generic sites are also important for these pedagogical issues. Erik, your studio on Concrete took on more everyday spaces, so maybe you could speak to that.

**Erik:** Yes, but they were also all quite beautiful architecturally and were rich enough to address politics, economics, history, in many different ways. But I think there's potential in looking even further beyond the monument, to develop alternative ways of reading buildings. My next studio is about systems and infrastructure, and how all of these systems relate to preservation. It's a dilemma, because suddenly we are left with no coherent monument, only continuities. It's harder to get. It's rich, but it's rich in a different way that is harder to detect.

**Bryony:** This is also an audience issue, because the questions around monuments are often easier for broader audiences to engage with than more technical or more banal architectural sites. Part of what was so exciting about the government project was how people actually cared, outside of the school, about what we were doing. There was a thrill to that and also a sense of meaning and depth. I'm just wondering about this question of audience, and if you all are thinking about getting preservation to matter to other audiences, to make it accessible.

One of the things I come across when I try to explain what experimental preservation is to people is that they often have trouble getting why that would be necessary. It's like the joke that you make, Jorge, that you don't want either your accountant or your preservationist to be experimental. If you're not invested in preservation discourse, it might seem odd to make preservation more experimental, since its purposes seem to be pretty clear. I think there is a challenge in terms of reaching other audiences, and I think the choice of sites also makes a difference in terms of how people get it or don't. So I'm curious to hear your thoughts on that.

**Jorge:** It seems to me that the stakes of any discipline are irrelevant to most people outside of that discipline. Like how a writer writes is not as important to most people as the novel that they get to read. Is yours a lament for greater public investment in the stakes that are of the discipline, or is there something else?

**Bryony:** I think preservation is really unique as a form of design. It's a design discipline that actually does directly involve stakeholders who are not often trained as architects or preservationists. I think that's what's exciting about it — you deal with sites that people are deeply invested in, for personal and cultural reasons. It has so much potential to bridge between academic and non-academic audiences. But I do think that there's a challenge in explaining experimental approaches. It's important to find broad backing for such projects, because getting preservation projects to happen seems to require a kind of community support or investment.

**Jorge:** I think that the question of pedagogy is one way to attack this issue. You have students coming in that have a background in other fields, and it's interesting to consider the kinds of objects that we present to them. When Erik was talking about infrastructure and systems, I was thinking that's a very different way of conceptualizing the monument than we typically use, where we're thinking of a monument as a standing object on the ground. That's really critical, because in fact the other thing you do as a preservationist is to conceptualize the object, and in a way that is not the same as let's say the original architect might have conceptualized it. So to take for instance the idea of a historic district, or of a viewshed, these are objects that cut across many people's properties that were never intentionally given as objects or conceptualized as objects until preservationists came and drew the line and began to argue for them as such.

So I think that Erik's studio is very interesting in that sense, because systems are potentially endless, so you have to draw a line around them somewhere and begin to conceptualize them as an object. That's where you have to bring in a discourse, a type of understanding. You begin to create and design an object out of parts that are already there, operating against many of the preconceptions that we have about what constitutes that object, such as its ownership, its transmission, its provenance. This is where I think in the last forty or fifty years preservation has begun to really separate itself from traditional art history or from traditional architecture in the sense that it's really begun to expand the meaning of an object.

**Thordis:** I think that's so interesting, and it really frames what we were discussing about preservation as a form of creation. What preservation is doing is again finding things and putting them together in a new way, whether it's a view or a system.

This makes me think of a ongoing project by the Swedish architectural office Spridd. It's not a preservation project, but it uses preservation tools to turn existing buildings into gold. They have taken a run-down 1960s slab block, but acted on it as something very special, by drawing it carefully, identifying everything about it very meticulously, and treating it as if it were a crucial, historical monument. They also have identified value in it that people didn't see before. So there we have architects acting as preservationists in some way on an object.

**Bryony:** It does seem to be an essential first step to conceptualize the type of creativity and the set of tools specific to this kind of practice. It's basically an amalgamation of the skills of economic strategy, structural analysis, material science, and architecture, and the ability to bring all of these together to remake an existing object.

**Thordis:** It's also through the act of drawing itself, through architectural drawing. Buildings that never have been drawn very carefully from the beginning, because they have been system buildings, are reframed just by creating a faithful and detailed representation of them.

# Teaching Bibliography

## Bryony Roberts

The following texts provide useful discussion points for seminar and studio courses on the transformation of existing architecture. Far from a comprehensive bibliography of preservation history or discourse, this selection instead prioritizes a critical questioning of how contemporary practices can frame historical buildings. Starting off with texts from Georges Bataille, Walter Benjamin, and Friedrich Nietzsche, this bibliography asks students to consider how preservation can reinforce or challenge institutions of cultural and political authority. That perspective prompts alternative readings of the following selected histories and primary sources of preservation. Moving to the intersection of preservation and design, the next series of texts prompts reevaluation of the prevalent concepts of contextualism and typology, and discussion of past strategies of intervention.

### Critical History
Bataille, Georges. "The Obelisk." In *Visions of Excess*. Edited and translated by Alan Stoekl, 213-21. Minneapolis: University of Minnesota Press, 1995.

Benjamin, Walter. "Thesis on the Philosophy of History." In *Selected Writings, Volume 4: 1938-1940*, edited by Howard Eiland and Michael W. Jennings, 389-97. Cambridge: Harvard University Press, 2003.

Nietzsche, Friedrich. "On the Utility and Liability of History for Life." In *The Nietzsche Reader,* edited by Keith Ansell Pearson and Duncan Large, 124-41. Oxford: Blackwell, 2006.

### Histories of Preservation
Arrhenius, Thordis. *Fragile Monument: On Conservation and Modernity.* London: Black Dog, 2012.

Bandarin, Francesco, and Ron van Oers. *The Historic Urban Landscape: Preserving Heritage in an Urban Century.* Oxford: Wiley-Blackwell, 2012.

Choay, Françoise. *The Invention of the Historic Monument.* Translated by Lauren M. O'Connell. Cambridge: Cambridge University Press, 2001.

Fitch, James Marston. *Historic Preservation: Curatorial Management of the Built World.* Richmond: University of Virginia Press, 1990.

Jokilehto, Jukka. *A History of Architectural Conservation.* London: Routledge, 2002.

Stanley-Price, Nicholas, M. Kirby Talley Jr., and Alessandra Melucco Vaccaro, eds. *Historical and Philosophical Issues in the Conservation of Cultural Heritage.* Los Angeles: Getty Conservation Institute, 1996.

Summerson, John. "Ruskin, Morris, and the 'Anti-Scrape' Philosophy." In *Historic Preservation Today,* 23-32. Richmond: University Press of Virginia, 1966.

### Primary Sources for Preservation
Boito, Camillo. "Restoration in Architecture: First Dialogue." Translated by Cesare Birignani. *Future Anterior* 6, no.1 (Summer 2009): 68-83.

de Quincy, Antoine Chrysostome Quatremère. "Restitution," "Restore," "Ruin." In *The True, the Fictive, and the Real: The Historical Dictionary of Architecture of Quatremère de Quincy.* Edited by Samir Younés, 217-22. London: Andreas Papadakis Publisher, 1999.

Ruskin, John. "The Lamp of Memory." In *The Seven Lamps of Architecture,* 167-87. New York: Farrar, Straus and Giroux, 1961.

Viollet-le-Duc, Eugene-Emmanuel. "Restoration." In *Historical and Philosophical Issues in the Conservation of Cultural Heritage.* Edited by Nicholas Stanley-Price, M. Kirby Talley Jr., and Alessandra Melucco Vaccaro, 314-18. Los Angeles: Getty Conservation Institute, 1996.

Viollet-le-Duc, Eugene-Emmanuel. "Style." In *The Foundations of Architecture: Selections from the Dictionnaire Raisonne.* Translated by Kenneth Whitehead, 230-63. New York: George Braziller, 1990.

### Contemporary Preservation Discourse

Allais, Lucia. "Disaster as Experiment: Superstudio's Radical Preservation." *Log* 22 (Spring/Summer 2011): 125-29.

Allais, Lucia. "International Style Heritage." *Volume* 20 (2009): 126-32.

Carpo, Mario. "The Postmodern Cult of Monuments." *Future Anterior* 4, no. 2 (Winter 2007): 51-60.

Diller, Elizabeth, Ricardo Scofidio, and Jorge Otero-Pailos. "Morphing Lincoln Center." *Future Anterior* 1, no. 1 (Summer 2009): 85-96.

Koolhaas, Rem. "Cronocaos." *Log* 21 (Winter 2011): 119-24.

Lima, Zeuler. "Preservation as Confrontation: The Work of Lina Bo Bardi." *Future Anterior* 2, no. 2 (Summer 2005): 25-31.

Lynch, Kevin. "The Presence of the Past." In *What Time Is This Place*, 29-64. Cambridge: MIT Press, 1972.

Otero-Pailos, Jorge. "Creative Agents." *Future Anterior* 3, no. 2 (Summer 2006): iii-vii.

Otero-Pailos, Jorge, Erik Langdalen, and Thordis Arrhenius, eds. *Experimental Preservation.* Zurich: Lars Müller Publishers, 2016.

Roberts, Bryony. "Competing Authenticities." *Future Anterior* 12, no. 2 (Winter 2015): 1-11.

Superstudio. "Salvages of Italian Historic Centers." *Log* 22 (Spring/Summer 2011): 114-25.

### Contextualism

Forty, Adrian. "Context." In *Words and Buildings*, 132-35. London: Thames & Hudson, 2000.

Frampton, Kenneth. "Prospects for a Critical Regionalism." *Perspecta* 20 (1983): 147-62.

Gregotti, Vittorio. "Territory and Architecture"and "The Exercise of Detailing." In *Theorizing A New Agenda for Architecture: An Anthology of Architectural Theory, 1965-1995.* Edited by Kate Nesbitt, 338-44, 494-97. New York: Princeton Architectural Press, 1996.

Gregotti, Vittorio. "On Modification." In *Inside Architecture.* Translated by Peter Wong and Francesca Zaccheo, 67-73. Cambridge: MIT Press, 1996.

Isenstadt, Sandy. "Contested Contexts." In *Site Matters: Design Concepts, Histories, and Strategies.* Edited by Carol J. Burns and Andrea Kahn, 157-79. New York:  Routledge, 2005.

Rogers, Ernesto. "Preexisting Conditions and Issues of Contemporary Building Practice." In *Architecture Culture 1943-1968.* Edited by Joan Ockman, 200-204. New York: Columbia University, 1993.

Rogers, Ernesto. "Evolution of Architecture." In *Architecture Culture 1943-1968.* Edited by Joan Ockman, 301-7. New York: Columbia University, 1993.

Rowe, Colin, and Fred Koetter. "Collage City and the Reconquest of Time," "Crisis of the Object: Predicament of Texture," "Collision City and the Politics of Bricolage." In *Collage City*, 118-50. Cambridge: MIT Press, 1979.

### Typology

Argan, Giulio Carlo. "On the Typology of Architecture." In *Theorizing a New Agenda For Architecture.* Edited by Kate Nesbitt. New York: Princeton Architectural Press, 1996.

Colquhoun, Alan. "Typology and the Design Method." *Arena, Journal of the Architectural Association* (June 1967).

Durand, J. N. L. *Precis des Lecons d'Architecture données à l'École polytechnique*, vol. XIII (Paris, 1805).

de Quincy, Antoine Chrysostome Quatremère. *The True, the Fictive, and the Real: The Historical Dictionary of Architecture of Quatremère de Quincy.* Edited by Samir Younés, 217-22. London: Andreas Papadakis Publisher, 1999.

Forty, Adrian. "Type." In *Words and Buildings*, 304-11. London: Thames and Hudson, 2000.

Moneo, Rafael. "On Typology." *Oppositions* 13 (Summer 1978): 23-45.

Moneo, Rafael. "Aldo Rossi: The Idea of Architecture and the Modena Cemetery." *Oppositions* 5 (1976): 1-30.

Rossi, Aldo. "from the *Architecture of the City*, 1966." In *Architecture Culture 1943-1968: A Documentary Anthology*. Edited by Joan Ockman with Edward Eigen, 392-98. New York: Columbia Books on Architecture/Rizzoli, 1993.

Rossi, Aldo. "An Analogical Architecture." In *Aldo Rossi: Selected Writings and Projects*. Edited by John O'Regan, 59-64. Architectural Design, 1983.

Vidler, Anthony. "The Third Typology." In *Architecture Theory Since 1968*. Edited by Michael Hays, 288-94. Cambridge: MIT Press, 1998.

### Intervention

Bishop, Claire, ed. *Participation*. London: Whitechapel, 2006.

Debord, Guy, and Gil Wolman. "Methods of Detournement." In *Situationist International Anthology*. Edited by Ken Knabb, 8-13. Berkeley: Bureau of Public Secrets, 1981.

Diller, Elizabeth, and Ricardo Scofidio. "The Withdrawing Room – A Probe Into the Conventions of Private Rite." *AA Files,* no. 17 (Spring 1989): 15-23.

Hollier, Denis. *Against Architecture*. Translated by Betsy Wing, 14-56. Cambridge: MIT Press, 1995.

Koolhaas, Rem. "Tabula Rasa Revisited." In *SMLXL*, 1090-1135. New York: Monacelli Press, 1995.

Kwon, Miwon. *One Place After Another : Site-Specific Art and Locational Identity*. Cambridge: MIT Press, 2004.

Lee, Pamela. "On the Holes of History." In *Object to Be Destroyed: The Work of Gordon Matta-Clark*, 162-209. Cambridge: MIT Press, 2001.

**AHO Re:Store Oslo Studio, Fall 2014**
Text by Andrea Pinochet

**GSAPP Oslo July 22 Studio, Fall 2014**
Text by Jorge Otero-Pailos

**The Polis: Reimagined**
Thesis Project by Kelsy Alexander

**The New Government Quarter—Other Teams**
Projects by Asplan Viak, BIG, LPO,
MVRDV, Snøhetta, and White

# Addendum

# AHO Re:Store Oslo Studio, Fall 2014

## Andrea Pinochet

**Teachers: Bryony Roberts, Andrea Pinochet, Laura Saether**
Students: Kelsy Alexander, Paul Bailey, Ines Bendelac, Trine Bølviken, Tommy Degerth, Bruguers Gallego-Guiu, Brit Heltne, Signe Ludvigsen, Ivana Mijic, Marcos Moreira, Eva Negård, Ida Nordstrøm, Halvor Saga, Miguel Saludas, Rebecca Schulz, Juris Strangots, Cecilie Sundt

In the fall of 2014, the Oslo Re-store course asked students to reimagine the government quarter of Oslo, which was damaged in the terrorist act of 2011. The studio, taught by Bryony Roberts, Laura Sæther, and myself, was conducted under the conceptual framework of *Experimental Preservation*, which entailed working with the existing structures while responding to the political and social history of the site.

From the outset, it was an ambitious activist endeavor that asked students to analyze and engage with the local debate by proposing reuse strategies for the future. In the first half of the semester, students conducted analytical research on the history of the government district, the genealogy of the site, and future development plans. Students also explored questions of politics, authorship, national identity, and memory. In the second half of the semester we asked students to propose a singular intervention addressing one of the many challenges the site faces today.

### The premise

Before the attack on July 22, 2011, Riksantikvar, the National Preservation authority of Norway, had been building a case for the protection of both the Høyblokka and the Y-blokka, which were designed by Norwegian modernist architect Erling Viksjø. After the attack, the media attention focused on the victims, the cleanup of the city, and the trial. Amidst the shock and the debris, it was assumed that the government buildings were too damaged and needed to be demolished. Rather quickly, numerous studies and evaluations emerged, turning the reconstruction into an opportunity for expansion, urban renewal, and economic development — almost without exception recommending the demolition of the Viksjø complex. But surprisingly, once the broken glass and damaged furnishings were removed, it became clear that the buildings were actually structurally intact, due to the strength of their unique concrete construction.

As we planned the studio, a debate over the fate of the Høyblokka gained strength in the media, polarizing various stakeholders. Architects, artists, and historians began to raise questions, reminding us of the quality of the building and of Viksjø's collaboartion with artists, including Picasso and several significant Norwegian artists. They testified to the cultural value of the building and warned against the irrevocable act of demolition.

### Preservation, a political question

During the first phase of the studio, we set up five research units. Every student was asked to produce an analytical document to be compiled in a book that not only became the basis for a mutual understanding of the problem in the studio, but also made the research available to the government planning organizations and local architecture and planning critics.

Just a couple of weeks before our studio began, the government announced the implementation of Konsept Øst (Concept East), a dense and compact massing scheme creating a unified compound on the eastern part of the site. Apart from dividing the center in two, this scheme entailed the demolition of some parts of the Høyblokka as well as the complete demolition of several other buildings, including the Y-blokka.

With the announcement of Konsept Øst, it became necessary for students to take a critical stance toward the proposal. The students considered how an architectural intervention could respond to the history of the place, the trauma of the attack, and programmatic needs of a new government expansion all at the same time. They also actively questioned whether these demands were compatible and realistic. Students argued for elements to "save" the quarter, then addressed all the challenges posed by the new programmatic and functional demands. Each student proposed a *parti*; a singular move or idea that guided their architectural intention.

Given the large amount of elements to consider, each student limited their intervention to one of the following areas: Høyblokka, Y-bløkka, the ground, or the urban plan. The projects are organized around these four areas. All the students stepped up to the challenge. Together, they worked on a wide range of issues and approaches to the problem, from small interventions to radical reorganizations of the site. In the following pages are the sixteen proposals.

Andrea Pinochet is an architect and Assistant Professor at the Oslo School of Architecture and Design.

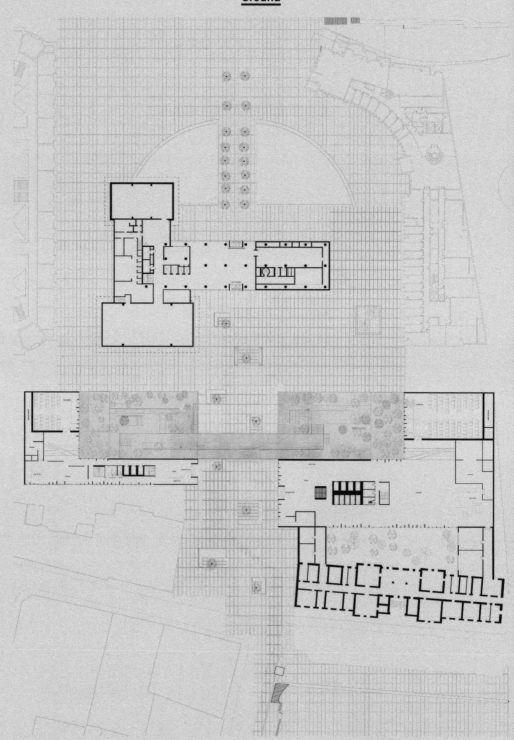

Signe Ludvigsen

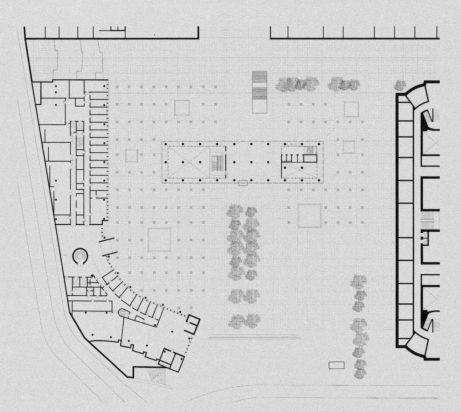

Cecilie Sundt and Ivana Miljic

Halvor André Saga

# Høyblokka

Eva Bakke Negård

Juris Strangots

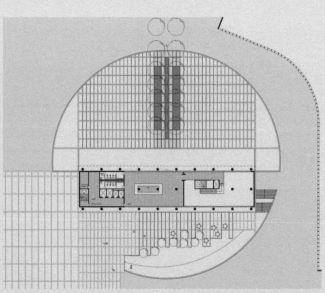

Marcos Moreira

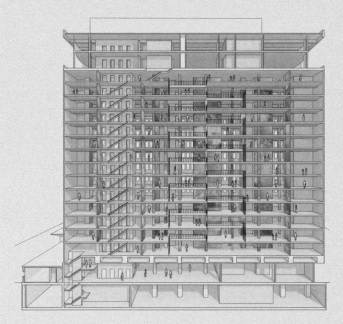

Trine Bølviken

Paul Bailey

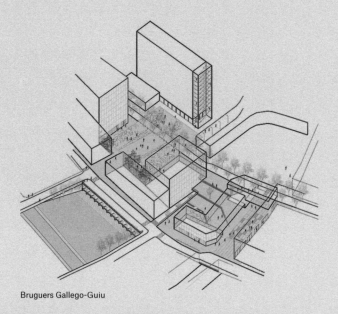

Bruguers Gallego-Guiu

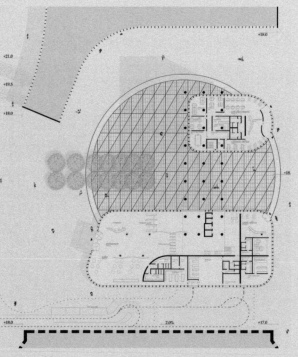

Miguel Saludas

Kelsy Alexander

Rebecca Schulz

# Y-blokka

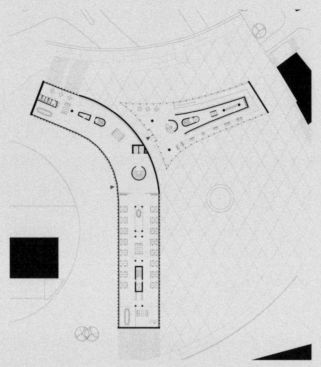

Brit Kristin Heltne

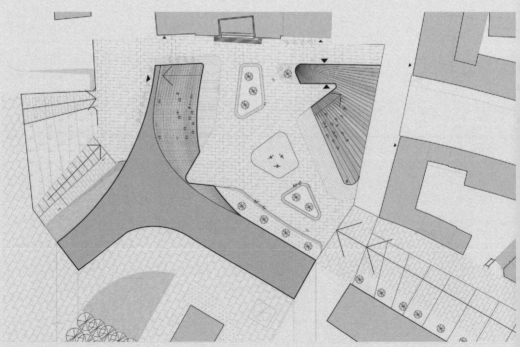

Tommy Degerth

Ida Nortstrøm

Ines Bendelac

# GSAPP Oslo July 22 Studio, Fall 2014

## Jorge Otero-Pailos

**Teachers: Jorge Otero-Pailos, Craig Konyk**
Students: Paridhi Agarwal, Diana Araujo, Xiaxiao Chen, Angel Garcia, Stephanie Jones, Wesley LeForce, Olimpia Lira, Carolina Llano, Michael Middleton, Anna Oursler, Kate Reggev, Andre Stiles

The targeting of symbols of power and governance in the form of significant works of architecture in significant locations in significant cities is a fairly recent phenomenon, one that is reoccurring with disturbing frequency worldwide. Our interest this semester will be the process of what comes next; what is the role of architects and urban designers in the design of an appropriate response? Like the quandary posed by the abrupt destruction of the World Trade Center Twin Towers, Oslo's officials and the larger population have struggled with what to do next. The fact that the Høyblokka survived structurally intact has made this quandary even more difficult. Should it be restored, with the renewed occupancy of government offices as a show of defiance? Or was this so traumatic an event that a different response is needed, one that veers towards memorialization of the victims and the site?

A competition for a temporary memorial for the site was held this year, and the schemes have been well received by the residents of Oslo. However, being temporary solutions, the ultimate determination of the final form and nature of the future use of the site is still an active discussion.

The task of the studio will be to propose the future use for the stabilized structure of Viksjø's Høyblokka, proposing how to reintegrate it into the life and fabric of today's post-Breivik Oslo. What is the most appropriate next architectural step, incorporating the latest theory of preservation and urban marking of events of major import? Complicating this issue is the existence of significant works by Picasso embedded within the architecture.

The studio will travel to Oslo in the third week of September, visiting the site and meeting with faculty and students of Oslo's AHO, the chief planner of Oslo, and members of the planning process for the government complex. Students will then propose solutions that incorporate all of these various difficult issues into a proposal for the future of the Høyblokka site.

Andre Stiles

Case Study: Addendum

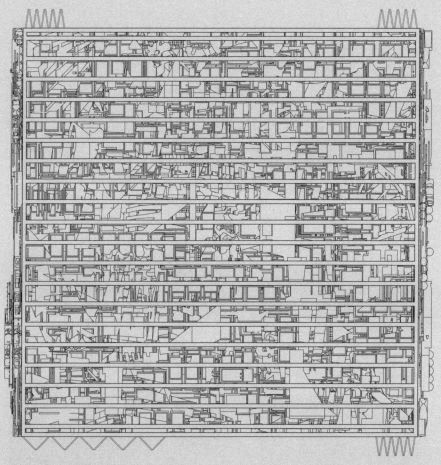

Wesley LeForce

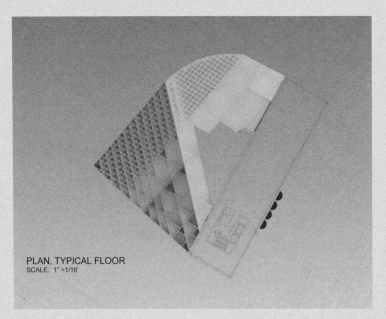

PLAN, TYPICAL FLOOR
SCALE: 1" =1/16'

Anna Oursler

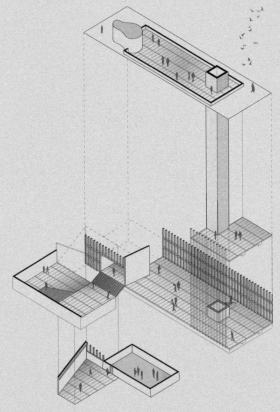

Stephanie Jones

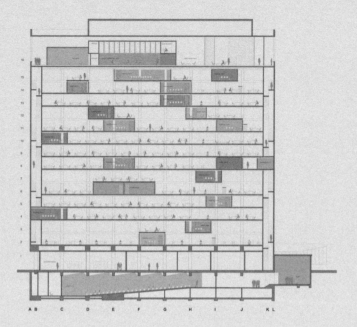

Olimpia Lira

Pari Agarwal

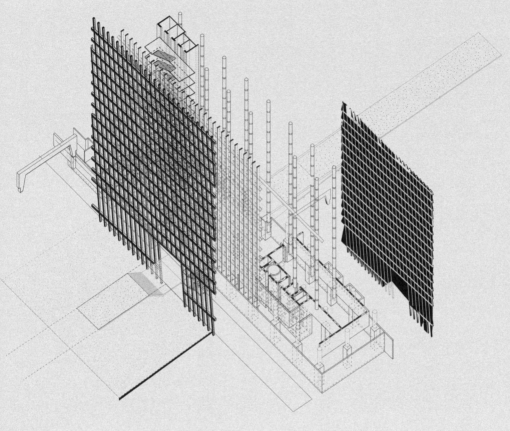

Carolina Llano

Diana Araujo

Michael Middleton

Kate Reggev

Xiaxiao Chen

# The Polis: Reimagined

## Kelsy Alexander

**Thesis Project at the Mackintosh School of Architecture, Glasgow, Spring 2015**

The political realm rises directly out of working together the sharing of words and deeds. Before men began to act a definite space had to be secured and a structure built where all subsequent actions could take place.

— Hannah Arendt, *The Human Condition*

The ancient Greek democratic system was based on a direct democracy, where every citizen with autonomy takes part in the democratic process of decision-making. In the Greek city-state the people (*demos*) were considered the absolute sovereign and this creates an autonomous political space. The public sphere was a place between individuals and the private government authorities in which people could meet, learn, and have critical debates about public matters.

Today, MPs and government officials are the agents of democracy, creating a disconnection between the public body and the State. How do we spatialize democracy in the twenty-first century? This thesis looks at reimagining the Greek model of democracy and adapting it to contemporary politics.

A void has been left in Oslo after the terrorist attack against the Norwegian government on July 22, 2011. There is now a need to restore the district. In an increasingly privatized built environment, architects must encourage viable open spaces for the contemporary polis.

By creating an open landscape for the public in which the lives of the public and private intertwine, public spaces are encouraged that stimulate political debate and conversation between different people. The architecture plays on empirical orders that have been reinterpreted for centuries, the temple, the gymnasia, the agora, the theater, in order to create a true democratic space.

Kelsy Alexander is an architect and former student at the Oslo School of Architecture and Design, while on exchange from the Mackintosh School of Architecture.

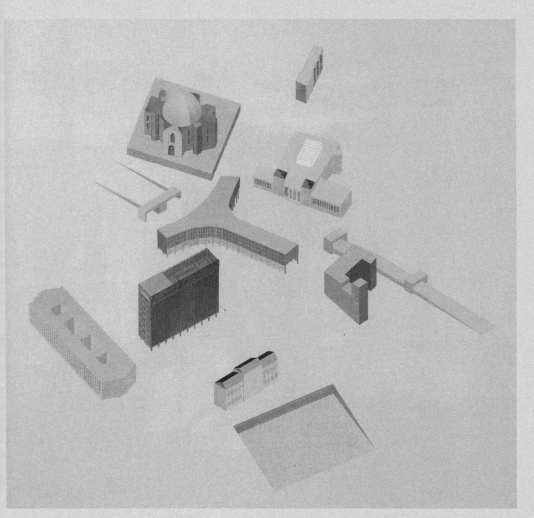

Existing monuments around a contested void

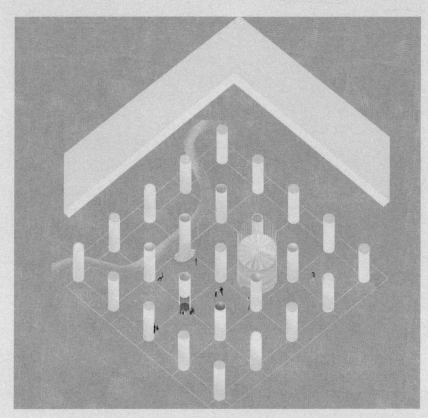

The polis reimagined

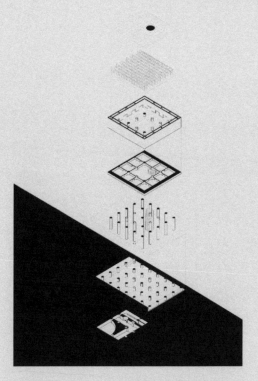

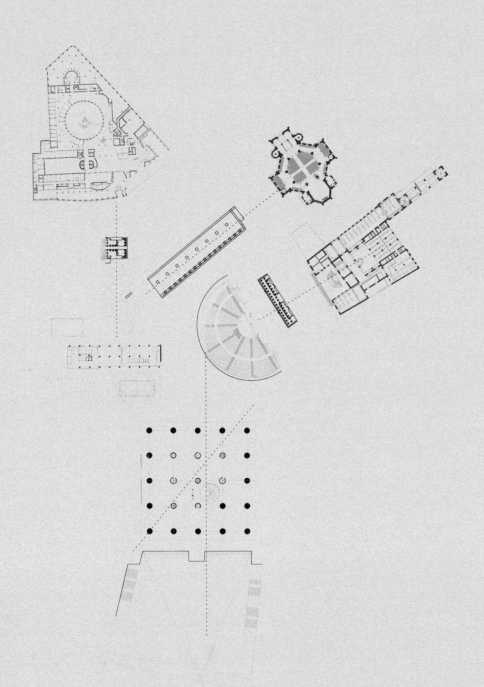

Site plan with new agora

# The New Government Quarter—Other Teams

## Projects by Asplan Viak, BIG, LPO, MVRDV, Snøhetta, and White

The Norwegian Directorate of Public Construction and Property (Statsbygg) invited six professional teams to submit master plans for the government quarter in Oslo. Each team was led by a large firm in collaboration with landscape architects and other consultants. The six teams were led by the offices of Snøhetta, MVRDV, Bjarke Ingels Group (BIG), White, LPO, and Asplan Viak.

In contrast to a typical competition, there would be no named winner of this ideas phase (parallelloppdrag), but rather ideas from each team would be integrated into a single zoning plan. After the completion of the zoning plan, however, architects would be invited to compete for the design of individual buildings. The potential of future commissions perhaps motivated the overscaled architectural ambitions and cooperation with the government's requirements visible in the following projects.

Team Asplan Viak, Government Garden, 2015

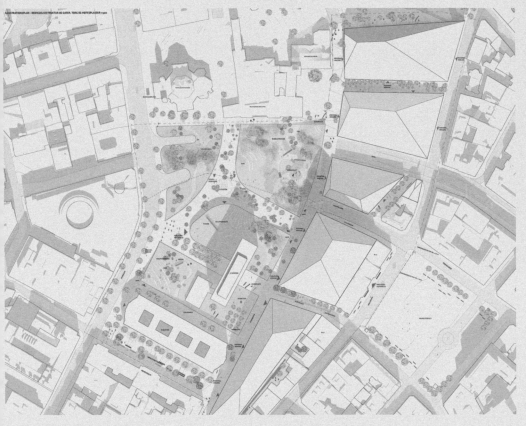

Team BIG, The People's Mountain, 2015

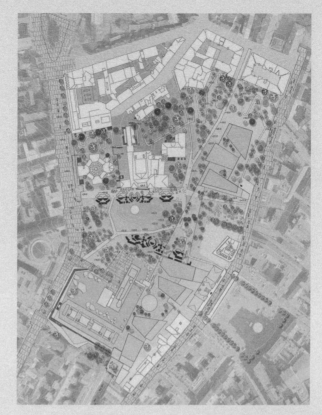

Team LPO, Government Quarter Hammersborg, 2015

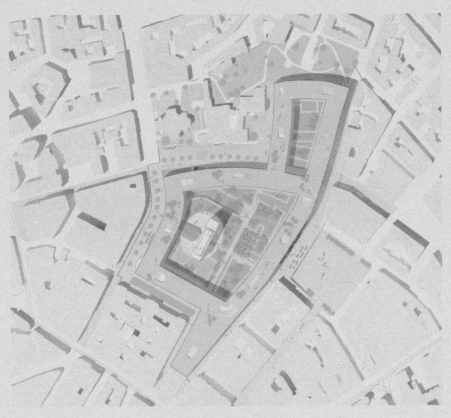

Team MVRDV, The Unifying Ring and the Norwegian Garden, 2015

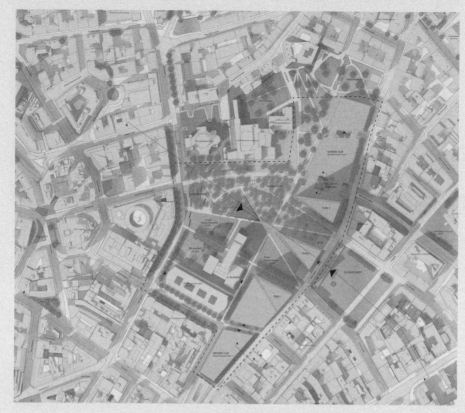

Team Snøhetta, Folk, 2015

Team White, A Place To Meet, 2015

Rally to save the Y-blokka,
February 9, 2015

## Image Credits